FOR ORGANS, PIANOS & ELECTRONIC KEYBOARDS

E-Z PLAY TODAY

299

THE VAUDEVILLE

T0044828

The Story, Stars and 25 Songs of Vaudeville

Article by David Fantle

ISBN 0-634-0110-8

HAL•LEONARD
CORPORATION

7777 W. BLUEMOUND RD. P.O. BOX 13819 MILWAUKEE, WI 53213

E-Z Play® Today Music Notation © 1975 by HAL LEONARD CORPORATION

Visit Hal Leonard Online at
www.halleonard.com

Table of Contents

The Place Where Stars Were Born

Before radio, before the movies could talk, and before television, there was vaudeville. Vaudeville was the king of entertainment for 60 years, from the last third of the nineteenth century until the early 1930s. Today, vaudeville is preserved in old photographs, rare recordings and film, and in memory by older Americans and the few vaudevillians who are still alive.

What do they remember? A time when two bits could buy nine acts of entertainment ranging from comic jugglers and Asian acrobats to dramatic monologues and one-act playlets. Vaudeville had something for everyone, and variety, more than anything else, was the secret to its success. It was also the best leisure-time deal around.

The fraternal community of vaudevillians included legendary stars that transcended the "two-a-day" to gain fame later in other mediums, most notably the Broadway stage, radio, television and motion pictures.

Many of the performers that appeared on the vaudeville stage have become part of the entertainment firmament. On any given night, from Altoona, Pennsylvania, to Zanesville, Ohio, audiences would be entertained by the antics of the Marx Brothers, the juggling prowess of W.C. Fields, the roping acumen and gentle humor of Will Rogers, the tapping feet of young Fred and Adele Astaire, the mesmerizing talent of legendary actress Sarah Bernhardt in a dramatic playlet, or the knock-em-in-the-aisle singing of Sophie Tucker.

For the talented (and lucky) few who made the transition to radio, motion pictures and television, vaudeville was an invaluable training ground, where songs, comic routines or dance numbers could be perfected before different audiences over the span of several years. Today's performers don't always have the luxury of refining an act; a single television appearance will expose the routine to an audience of millions and immediately can become stale.

The names of most vaudevillians have drifted into show business oblivion. The appeal of novelty acts such as Fink's Mules, Singer's Midgets and Swain's Cats and Rats could only have thrived in vaudeville, where a variety of acts were required to "fill the bill." In Swain's routine, rats dressed in tiny jockey uniforms would race on the backs of felines, much to the audience's amusement.

Beginnings

The word vaudeville originated in the Vire River Region in France, where Val de Vire was often pronounced "Vaude Vire," which became to mean "lively songs." Vaudeville was first used as a term in the United States in 1840 when a Boston establishment called itself a "Vaudeville Saloon" to promote a variety show. Vaudeville slowly began to take hold in the latter part of the century as British style music-hall and minstrel shows began to wane in popularity. Up to this time the theater was the domain of males and females of questionable repute.

Early vaudeville was basically a minstrel show stripped of the burnt cork that performers would use to "black up." (Throughout the duration of vaudeville, some performers such as Al Jolson and Eddie Cantor continued to perform in blackface.)

One man, Tony Pastor (born Antonio Pastore) is generally regarded as the "father of vaudeville." A former circus and minstrel performer, Pastor opened his first variety theater in Paterson, New Jersey, in 1865. Determined to clean up the image of stage entertainment, Pastor eliminated smoking and drinking in the theater, forbid off-color humor, and covered the female performers with costumes that exposed nothing. He even enticed female patrons by giving away groceries, kitchenware, dress patterns, and toys as door prizes.

The gimmicks worked and vaudeville gained in acceptability, attracting larger and more diverse audiences and eventually becoming the entertainment of choice for the masses. Pastor's Music Hall Theater opened in New York in 1881 and soon became the leading vaudeville theater in America.

Concurrent with vaudeville was another popular form of entertainment, burlesque. Originating in 1869, burlesque was the risqué cousin of vaudeville, where girls in tights caused a furor and "blue" humor was the order of the day. Many vaudevillian comics and singers, including Fanny Brice, W.C. Fields, Bert Lahr, and Sophie Tucker, got their start in burlesque.

The Heyday

The popularity of vaudeville quickly spread beyond Pastor's theater. Another circus veteran, B.F. Keith opened several theaters, and in the 1890s, partnered with E.F. Albee to start a chain of 70 theaters nationwide. In 1907, F.F. Proctor joined Keith and Albee and their empire grew. These vaudeville impresarios created circuits putting together a roster of talent that traveled throughout the country for years playing the various theaters, without ever having to change their act. Other circuits, with the names Orpheum, Pantages, and Gus Sun also flourished. A standard vaudeville bill typically would appear in a city for one week and then travel to another theater in the circuit.

Big-time vaudeville, or the two-a-day (meaning two performances a day), was the pinnacle for all vaudevillians. It meant lavish theaters, first class accommodations, humane working conditions, and high salaries. But it was not an easy climb to the top. The vast majority of vaudevillians languished in small-time theaters giving as many as 12 shows a day in something less than ideal conditions.

The Palace

In show business lore, no theater attained the legendary status or epitomized big-time vaudeville more than the Palace in New York City, for it was every vaudevillian's dream to one day perform in front of its footlights. The Palace opened in 1913, and soon became the preeminent vaudeville showhouse in the country and the jewel in B.F. Keith's circuit. The brainchild of producer Martin Beck, the Palace featured comedian Ed "The Perfect Fool" Wynn on its first bill.

With the Palace as the flagship theater, vaudeville entered its golden period. Approximately 2,000 theaters throughout the United States and Canada were dedicated to vaudeville. At its peak in the teens, it was estimated that 10 people attended a vaudeville show for every one who patronized another form of entertainment. In addition, vaudeville headliners were the highest paid people in the world. For example, stars such as Eva Tanguay earned $3,500 a week, Al Jolson, $2,500, and the Marx Brothers a staggering $10,000 a week.

The Tin Pan Alley Connection

As the number of theaters grew, so did the demand for Tin Pan Alley's songwriters, who were required to supply a steady stream of new material for vaudeville's many musical stars. Vaudeville was a song publisher's dream. By performing the popular songs of the day, every musical performer became a song plugger. And the shelf life of a song was extended as a performer criss-crossed the country performing the same repertoire. It's no wonder publishers could track where a performer was playing because of the sudden upswing in sheet music sales from that particular city.

Irving Berlin, the prolific composer and consummate marketer of his own music, actually played the vaudeville boards. In 1919, with Harry Akst at the piano, he sang some of his own compositions, including the World War I hit, "Oh How I Hate to Get Up in the Morning" and "Mandy."

Black Vaudeville

Few black performers were able to make the transition to big-time vaudeville. They appeared in "black vaudeville," a "poor relation" to the entertainment that reached white Americans. Bert Williams, Buck and Bubbles, and Bill "Bojangles" Robinson, were the few exceptions. Although they appeared on the "white stage," they were not allowed to eat in the same restaurants or sleep in the same hotels as their white counterparts. And an even worse indignity was given to the black audience members who were relegated to the farthest reaches of the balcony.

The Death Knell

By the early '30s, attendance began to decline. Radio and "talkies" were quickly displacing vaudeville as the new entertainment choice for the masses during the Depression. Why would people go to the neighborhood vaudeville theater when its practitioners such as Burns and Allen, Jack Benny and Fred Allen could be heard on the radio in the comfort of the family living room — and at no cost? Few Depression-era Americans could afford to spend their disposable income on entertainment. The unofficial death of vaudeville occurred Nov. 16, 1932: the Palace ended its two-a-day policy, using entertainers to supplement its daily presentation of feature length films.

Vaudeville continued to limp along until, by the end of the '30s, virtually every theater abandoned its vaudeville-only policy. Reincarnations of vaudeville-style performances continued to crop up on early television shows, most notably Milton Berle's "Texaco Star Theater," "The Ed Sullivan Show" and "The Colgate Comedy Hour."

Even today, novelty acts such as jugglers, ventriloquists, and impersonators occasionally pick up work in Las Vegas or Atlantic City — the last vestiges of vaudeville style acts. The venerable old Palace still exists, now playing host to Broadway shows. "The Will Rogers Follies," a revue in the spirit of Florence Ziegfeld, paid tribute to the late vaudevillian and enjoyed a long run at the Palace.

A century after its birth, the vaudeville tradition is virtually gone. Will the television-dominated American culture ever again return to the thrills of coast to coast live perfomances?

After You've Gone

Registration 8
Rhythm: Swing

Words by Henry Creamer
Music by Turner Layton

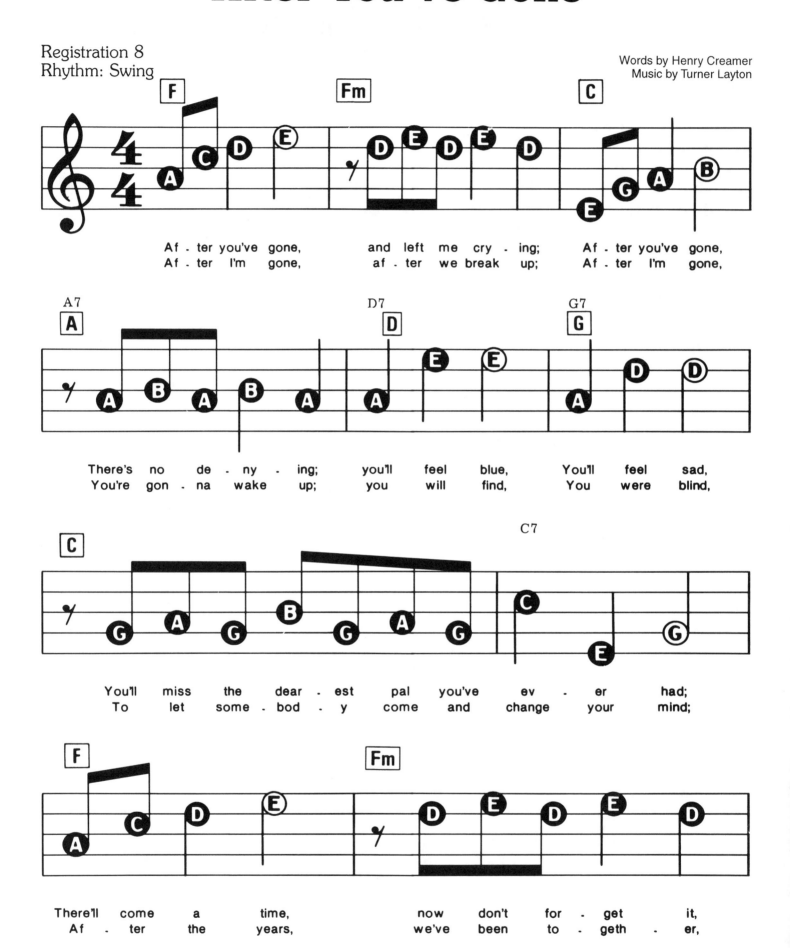

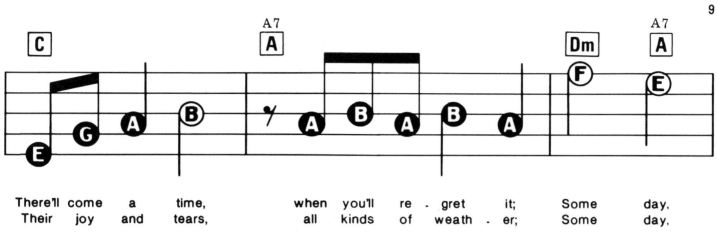

There'll come a time, when you'll re - gret it; Some day,
Their joy and tears, all kinds of weath - er; Some day,

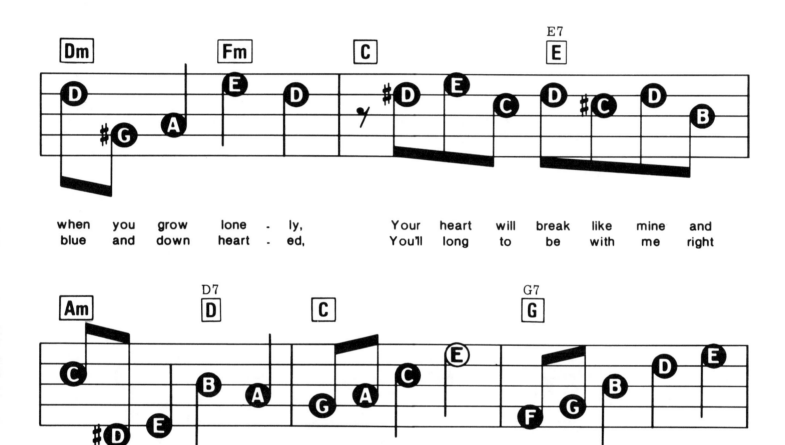

when you grow lone - ly, Your heart will break like mine and
blue and down heart - ed, You'll long to be with me and right

you'll want me on - ly, Af - ter you've gone, Af - ter you've gone a -
back where you start - ed; Af - ter I'm gone, Af - ter I'm gone a -

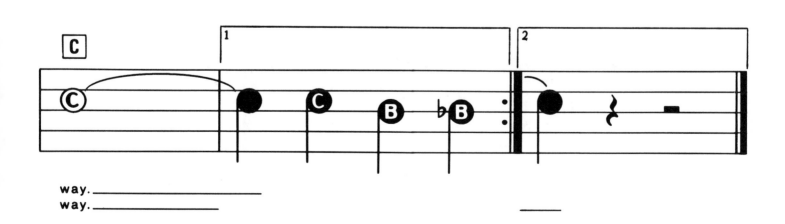

way. _____
way. _____

April Showers

Registration 9
Rhythm: Swing

Words by B.G. DeSylva
Music by Louis Silvers

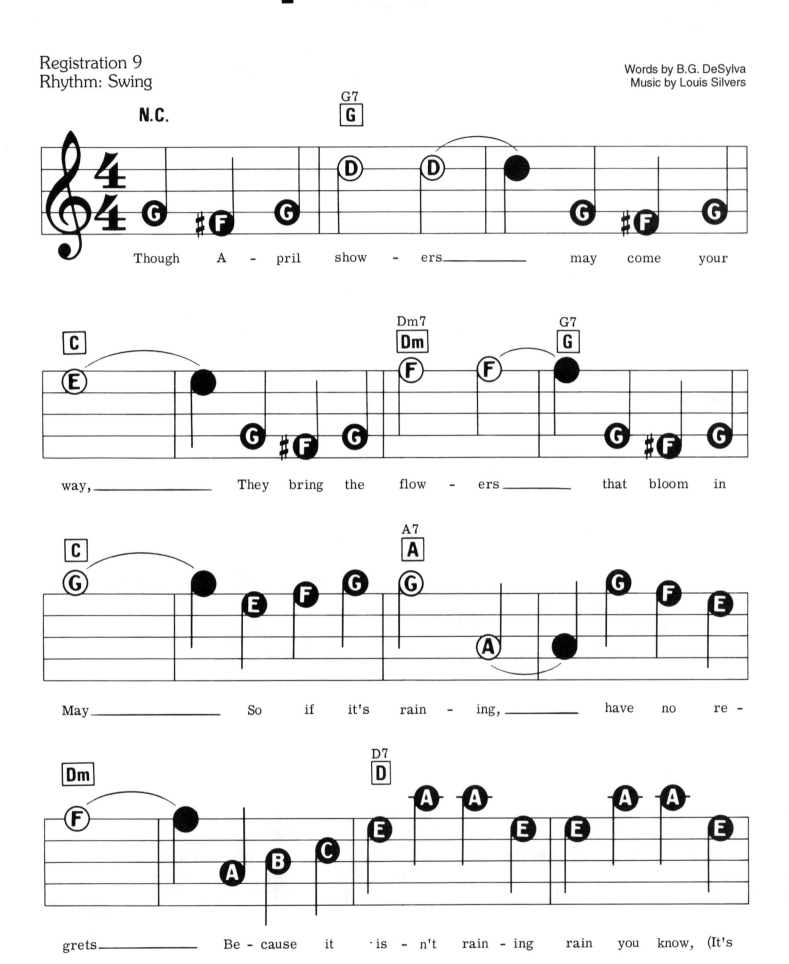

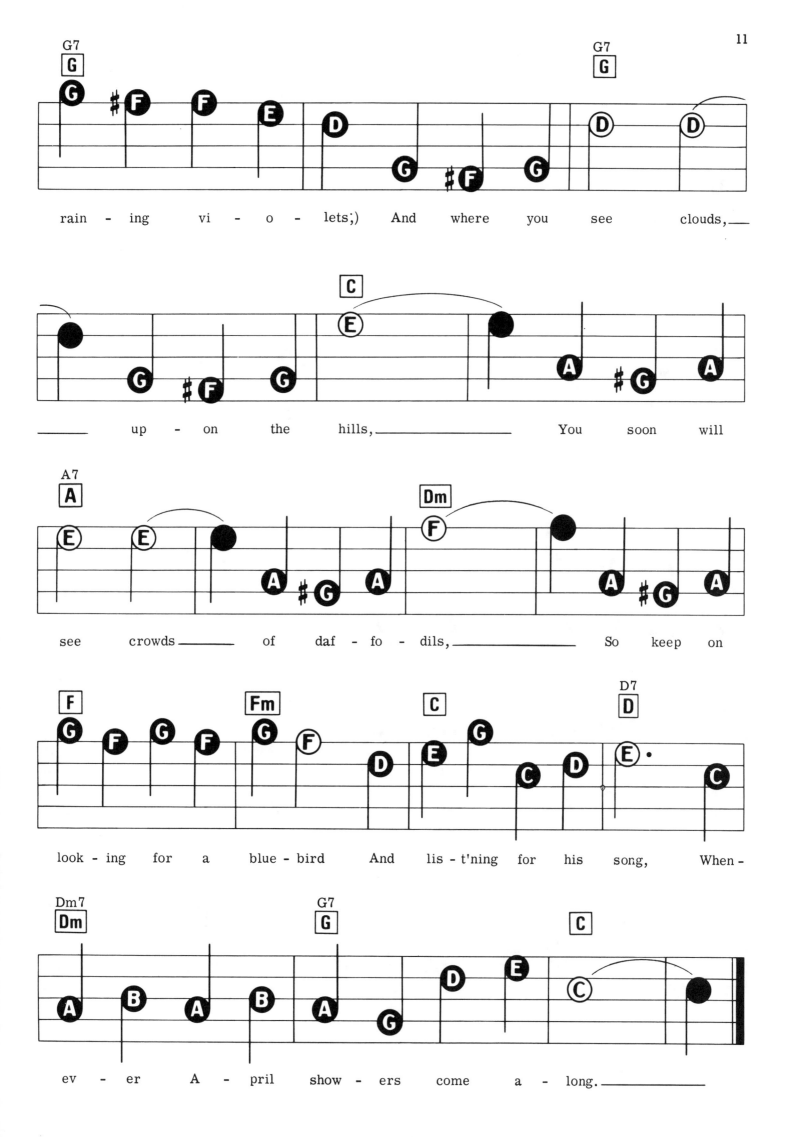

Ballin' the Jack

Registration 9
Rhythm: Swing or Fox Trot

Words by Jim Burris
Music by Chris Smith

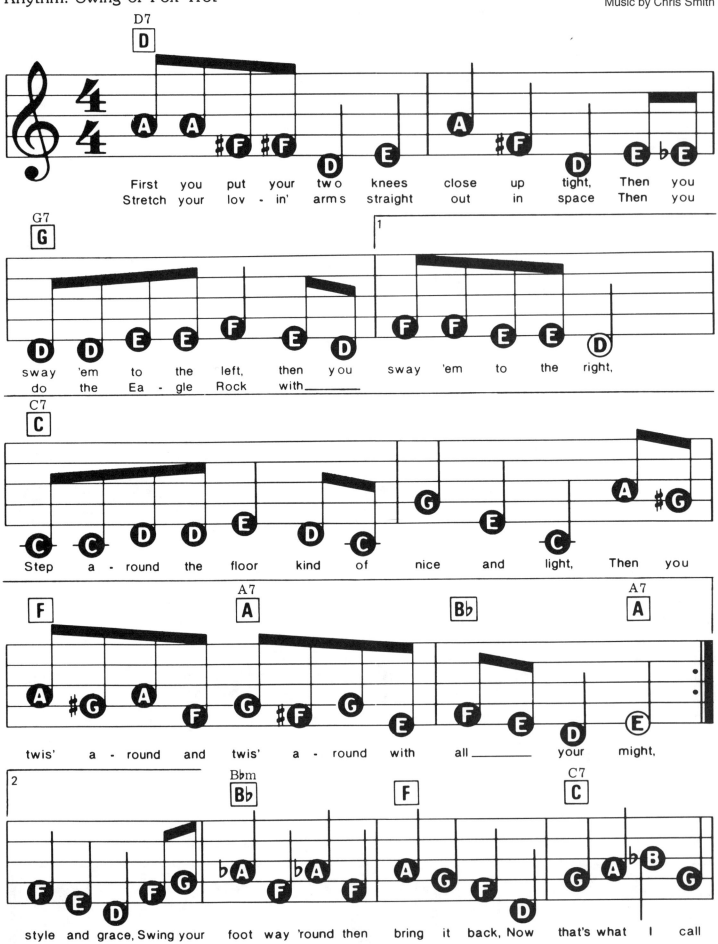

First you put your two knees close up tight, Then you
Stretch your lov - in' arms straight out in space Then you

sway 'em to the left, then you sway 'em to the right,
do the Ea - gle Rock with_____

Step a - round the floor kind of nice and light, Then you

twis' a - round and twis' a - round with all_____ your might,

style and grace, Swing your foot way 'round then bring it back, Now that's what I call

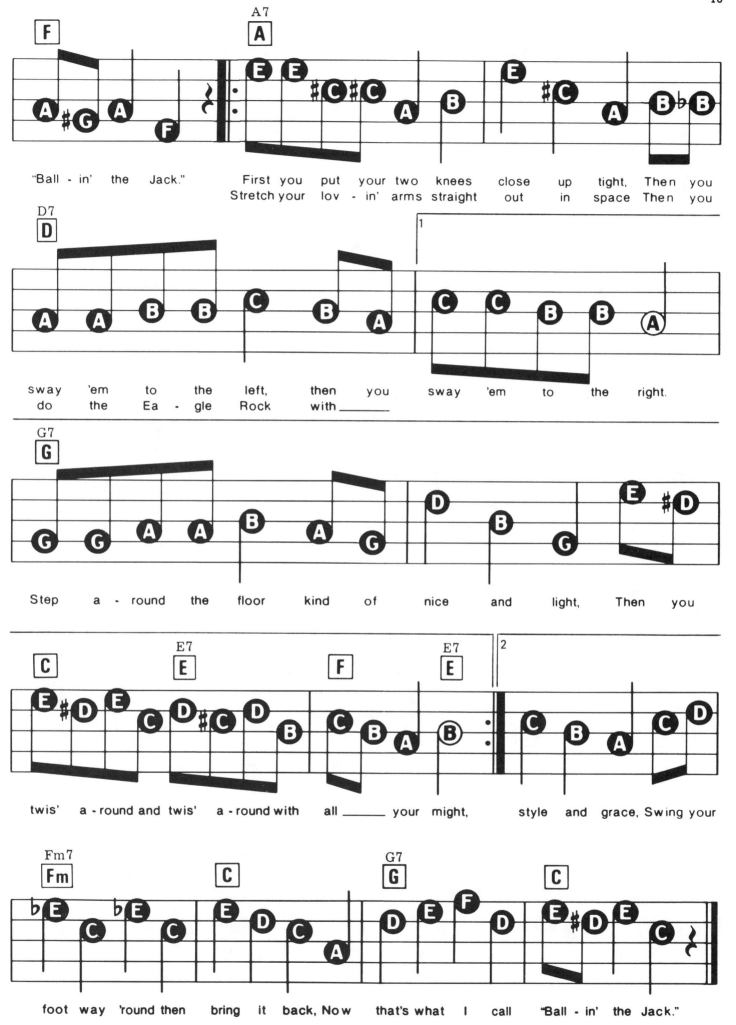

Bill Bailey, Won't You Please Come Home

Registration 7
Rhythm: Swing

Words and Music by
Hughie Canon

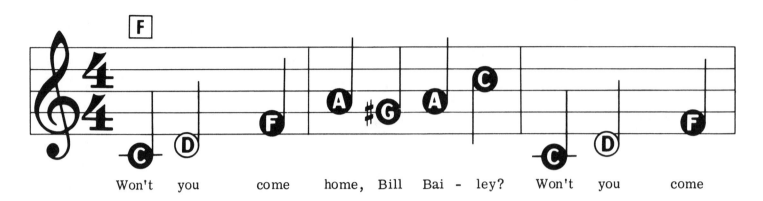

Won't you come home, Bill Bai - ley? Won't you come

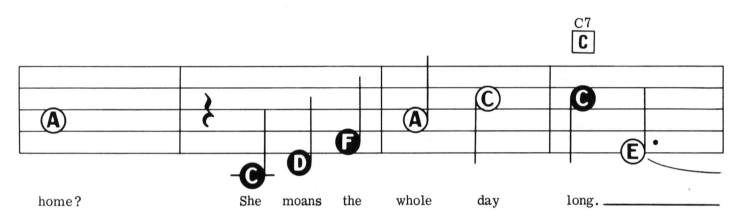

home? She moans the whole day long. _____

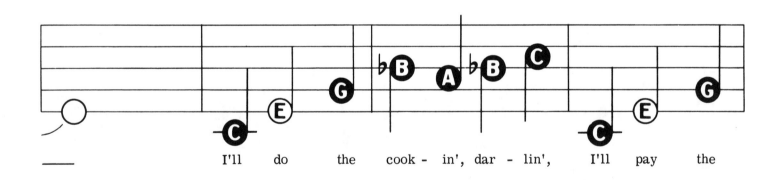

_____ I'll do the cook - in', dar - lin', I'll pay the

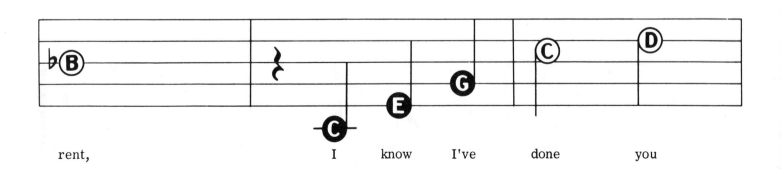

rent, I know I've done you

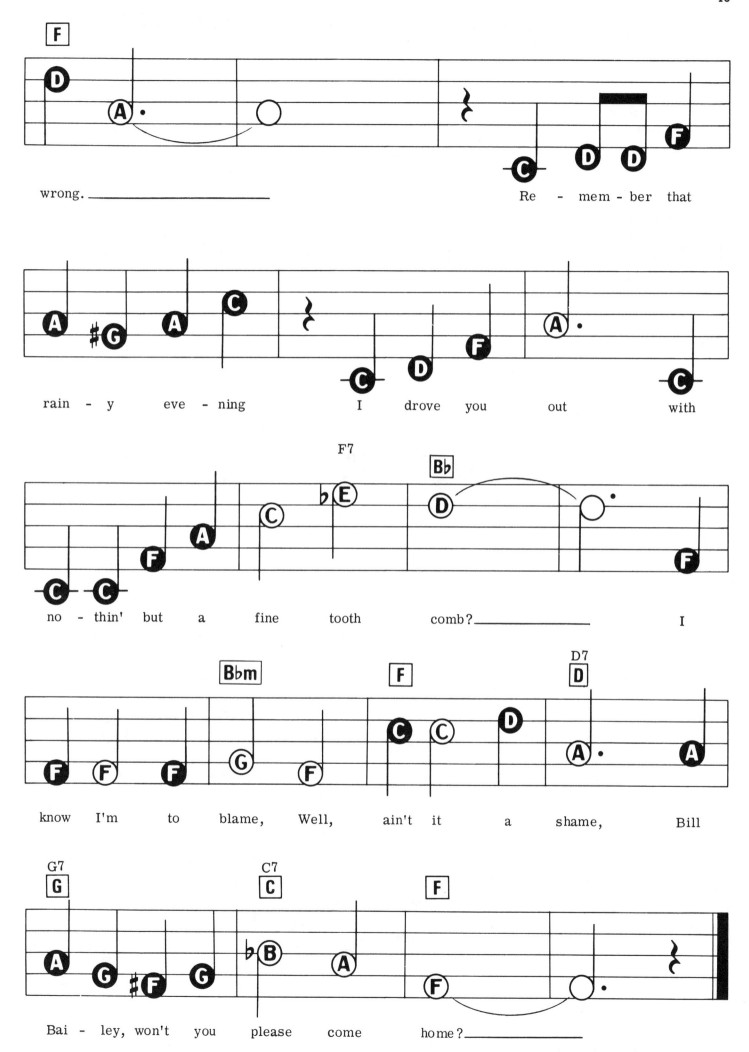

Chinatown, My Chinatown

Registration 4
Rhythm: Swing

Words by William Jerome
Music by Jean Schwartz

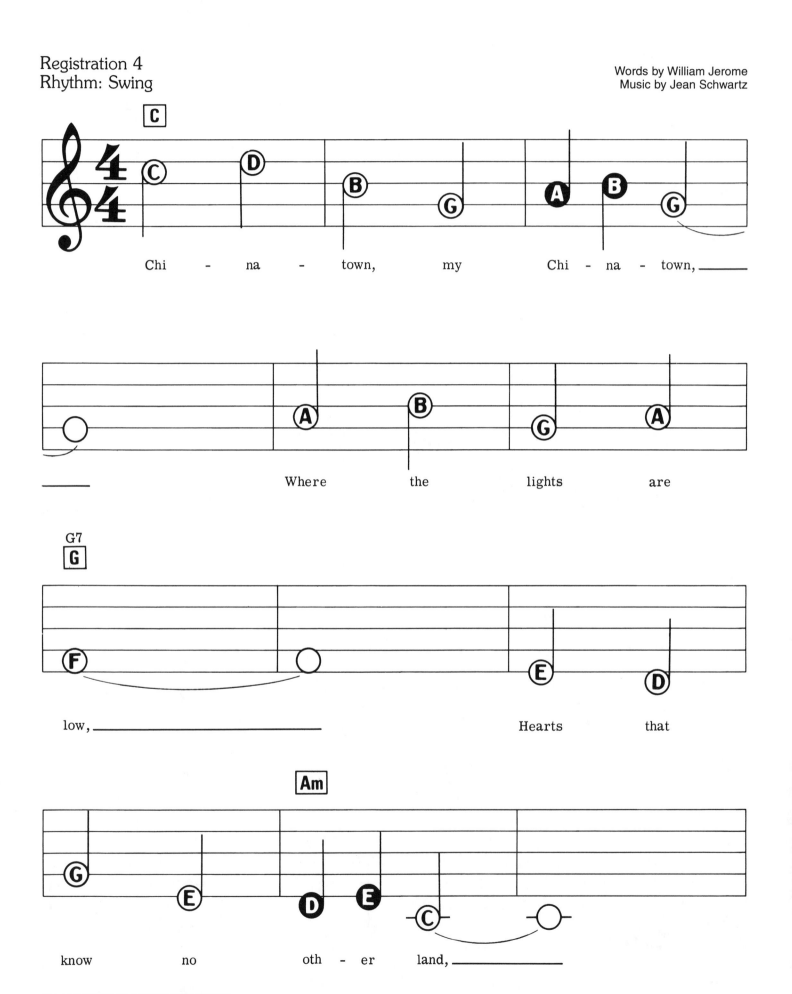

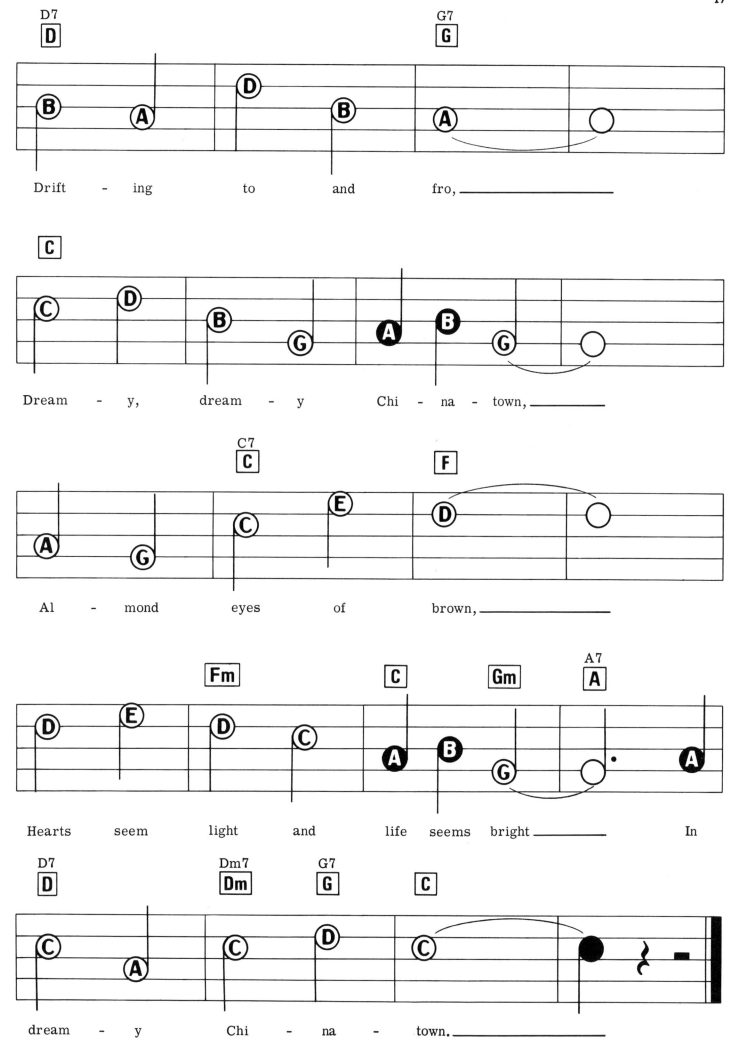

The Darktown Strutters' Ball

Registration 8
Rhythm: Polka, Fox-Trot, or Dixie

Words and Music by
Shelton Brooks

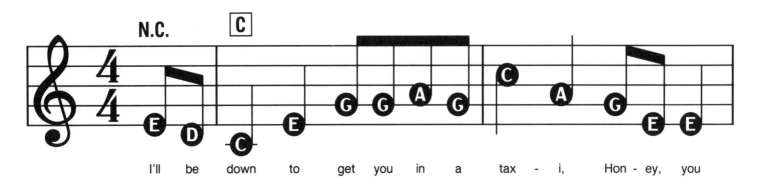

I'll be down to get you in a tax - i, Hon - ey, you

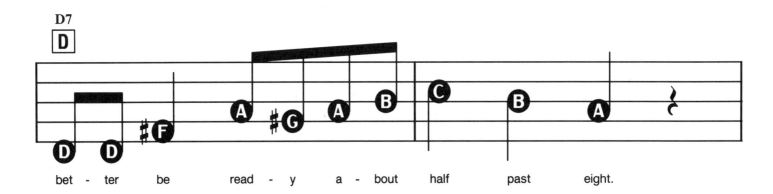

bet - ter be read - y a - bout half past eight.

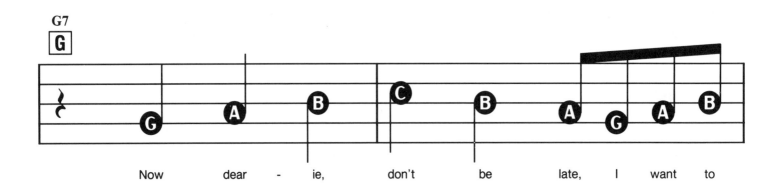

Now dear - ie, don't be late, I want to

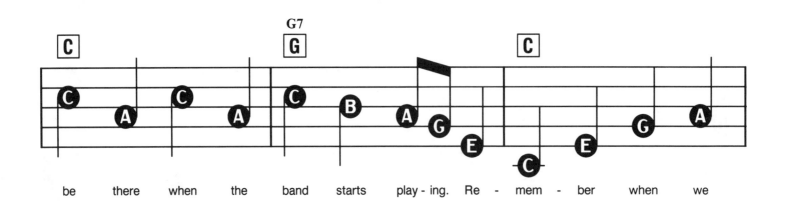

be there when the band starts play - ing. Re - mem - ber when we

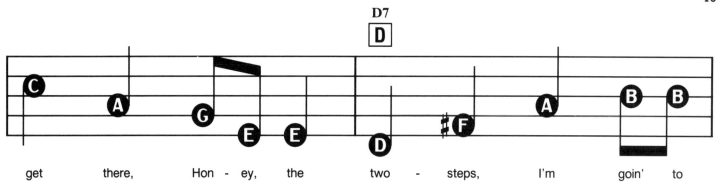

get there, Hon - ey, the two - steps, I'm goin' to

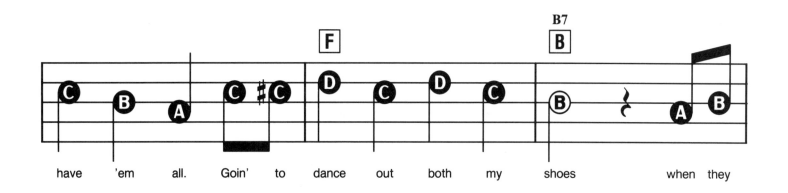

have 'em all. Goin' to dance out both my shoes when they

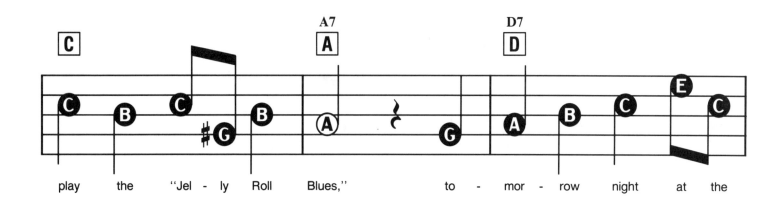

play the "Jel - ly Roll Blues," to - mor - row night at the

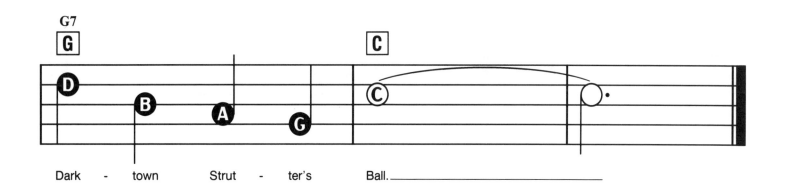

Dark - town Strut - ter's Ball.

Everybody's Doin' It Now

Registration 8
Rhythm: Swing

Words and Music by
Irving Berlin

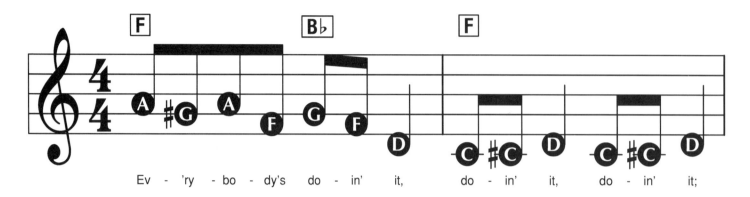

Ev - 'ry - bo - dy's do - in' it, do - in' it, do - in' it;

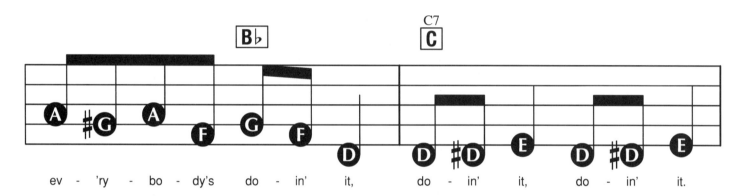

ev - 'ry - bo - dy's do - in' it, do - in' it, do - in' it.

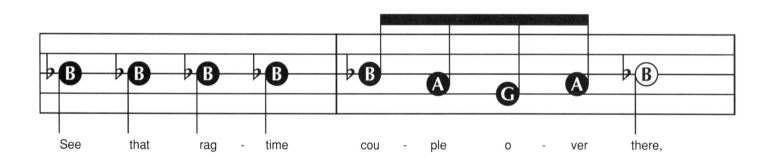

See that rag - time cou - ple o - ver there,

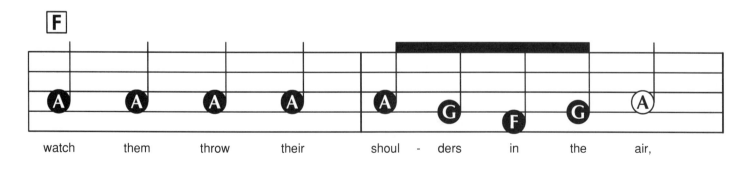

watch them throw their shoul - ders in the air,

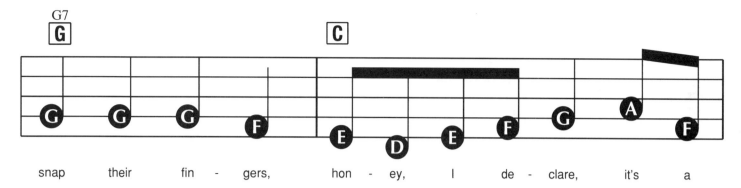

snap their fin - gers, hon - ey, I de - clare, it's a

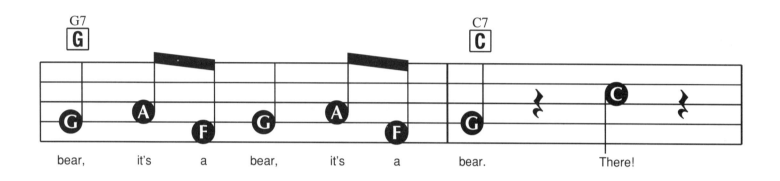

bear, it's a bear, it's a bear. There!

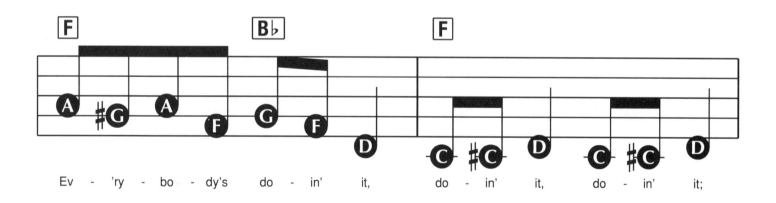

Ev - 'ry - bo - dy's do - in' it, do - in' it, do - in' it;

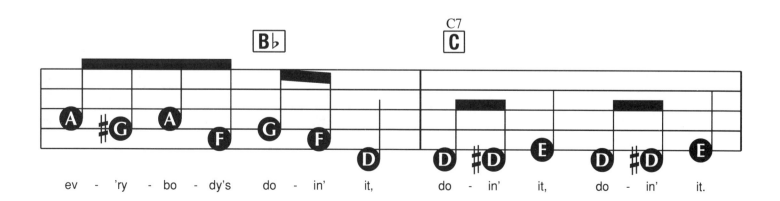

ev - 'ry - bo - dy's do - in' it, do - in' it, do - in' it.

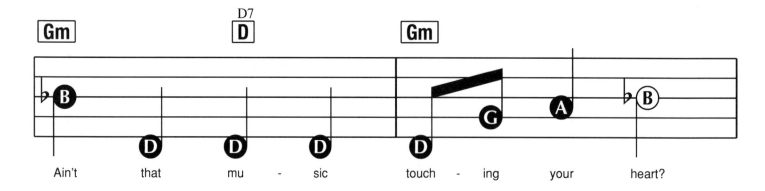

Ain't that mu - sic touch - ing your heart?

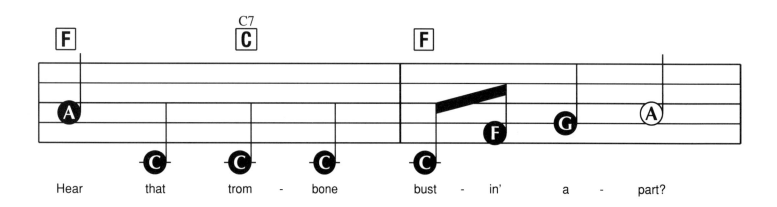

Hear that trom - bone bust - in' a - part?

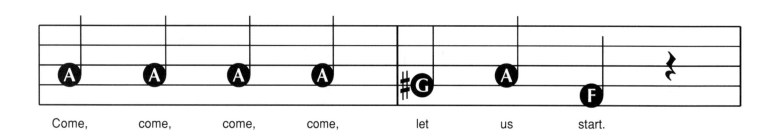

Come, come, come, come, let us start.

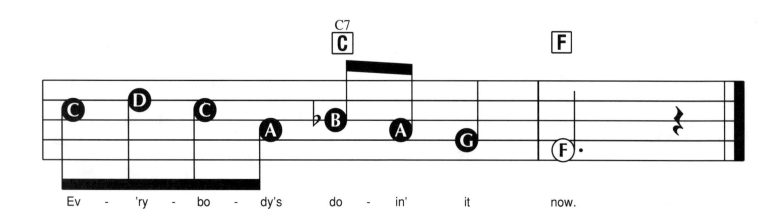

Ev - 'ry - bo - dy's do - in' it now.

How 'Ya Gonna Keep 'Em Down on the Farm?
(After They've Seen Paree)

Registration 8
Rhythm: March

Words by Sam M. Lewis and Joe Young
Music by Walter Donaldson

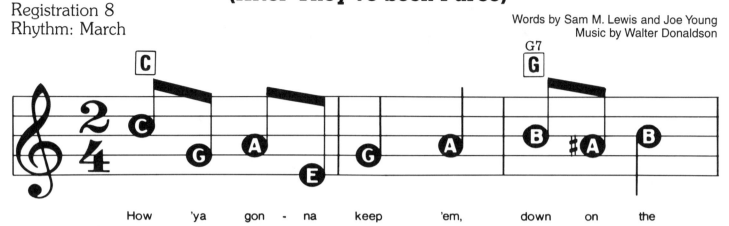

How 'ya gon - na keep 'em, down on the

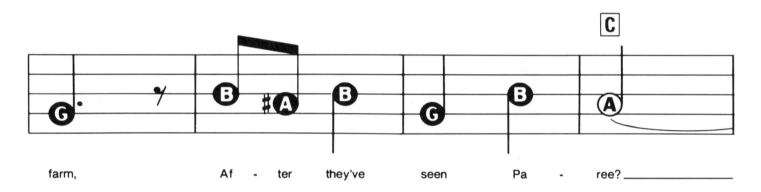

farm, Af - ter they've seen Pa - ree? _____

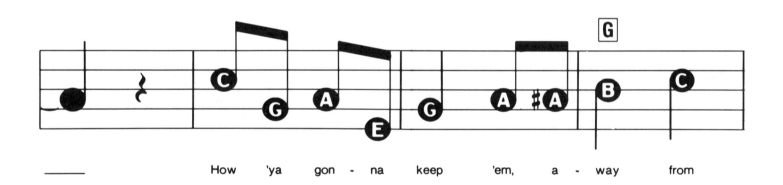

_____ How 'ya gon - na keep 'em, a - way from

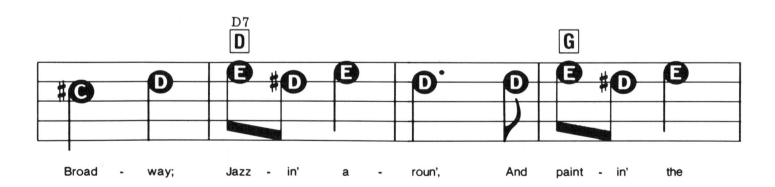

Broad - way; Jazz - in' a - roun', And paint - in' the

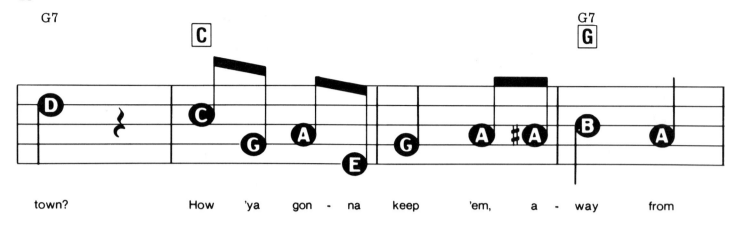

town? How 'ya gon - na keep 'em, a - way from

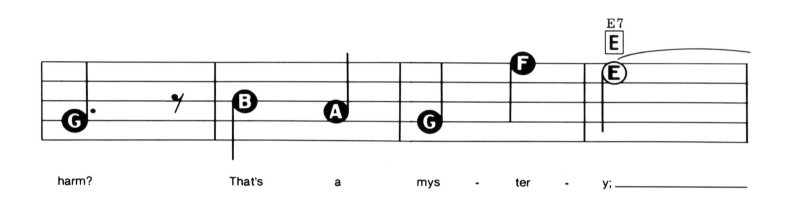

harm? That's a mys - ter - y; _____

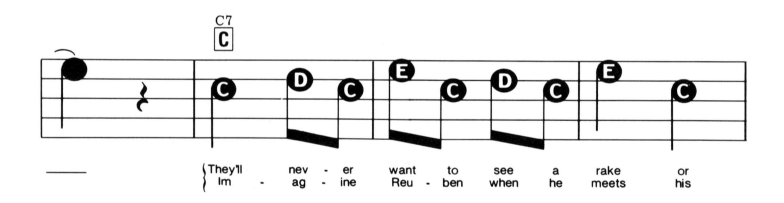

_____ {They'll nev - er want to see a rake or
{Im - ag - ine Reu - ben when he meets his

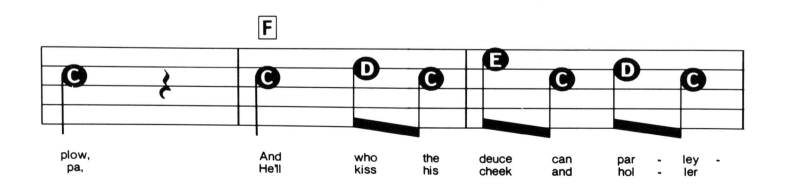

plow, And who the deuce can par - ley -
pa, He'll kiss his cheek and hol - ler

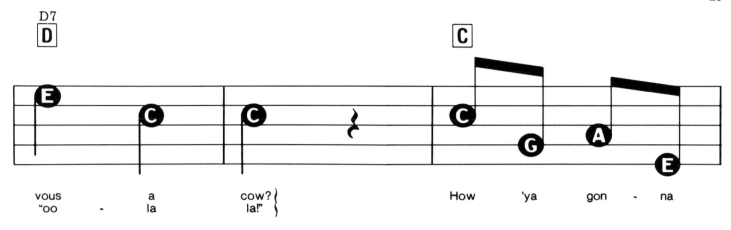

vous - a cow?
"oo - la la!"

How 'ya gon - na

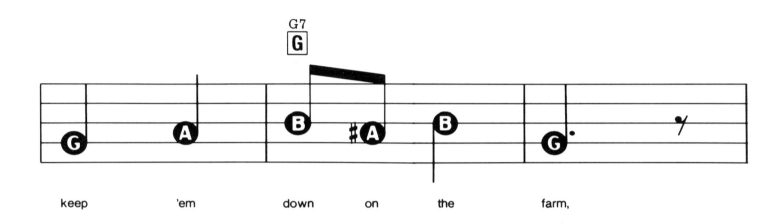

keep 'em down on the farm,

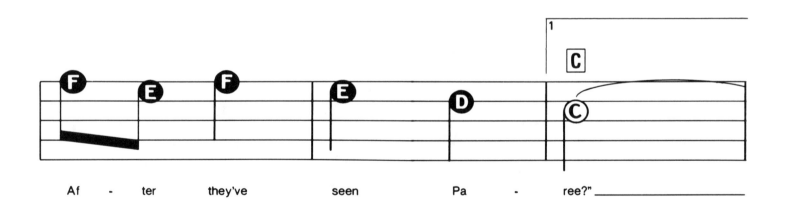

Af - ter they've seen Pa - ree?"_____

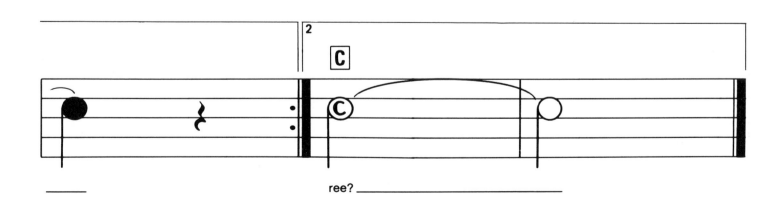

_____ ree?_____

A Good Man Is Hard to Find

Registration 5
Rhythm: 2-Beat, Swing, or Shuffle

Words and Music by
Eddie Green

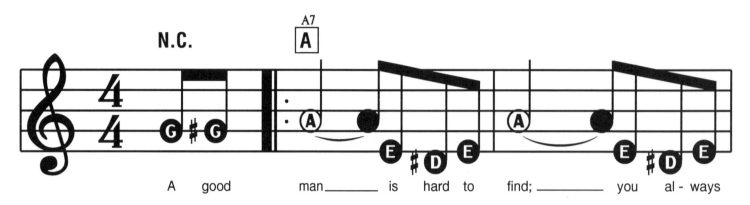

A good man is hard to find; you al-ways

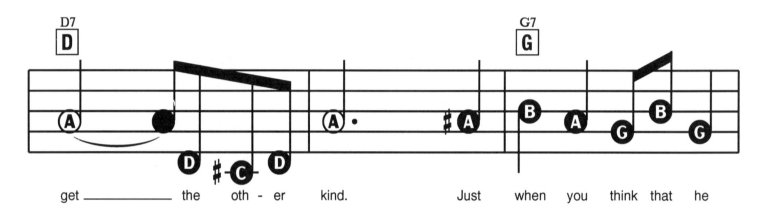

get the oth - er kind. Just when you think that he

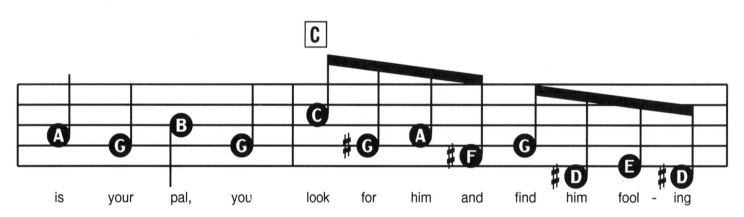

is your pal, you look for him and find him fool - ing

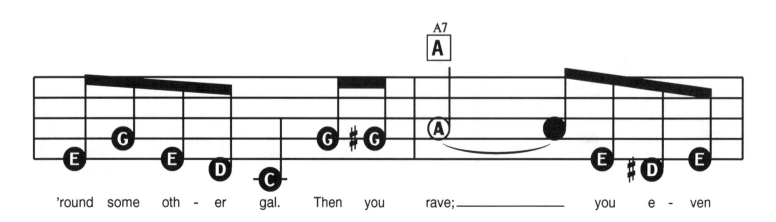

'round some oth - er gal. Then you rave; you e - ven

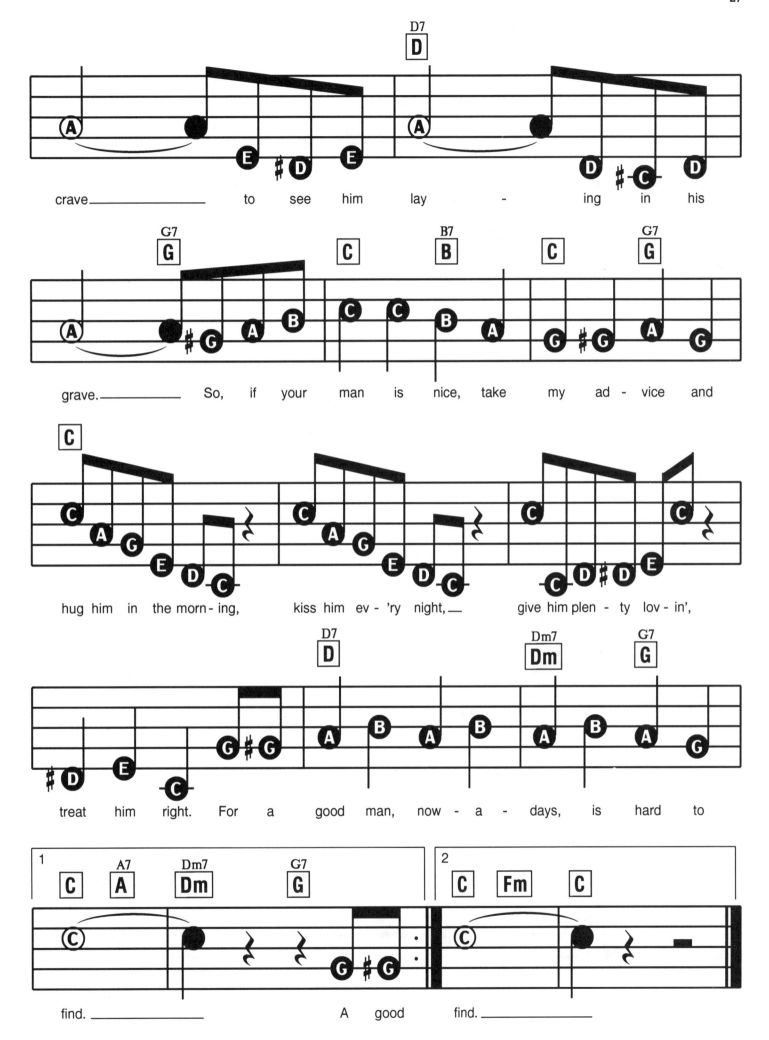

Hello! Ma Baby

Registration 7
Rhythm: Swing

Words by Ida Emerson
Music by Joseph E. Howard

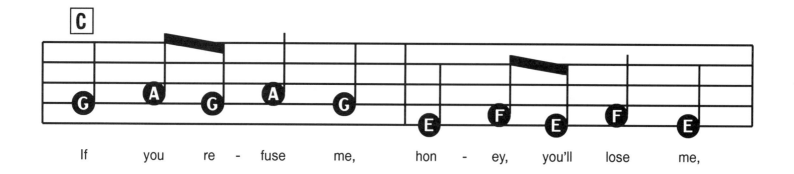

If you re - fuse me, hon - ey, you'll lose me,

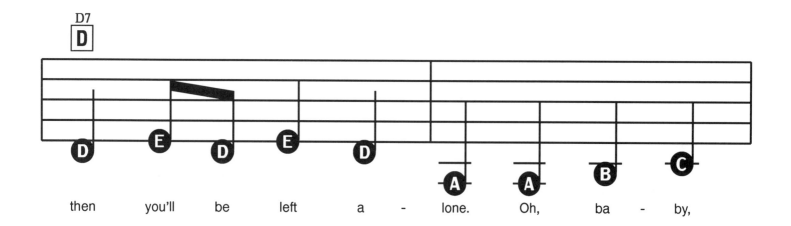

then you'll be left a - lone. Oh, ba - by,

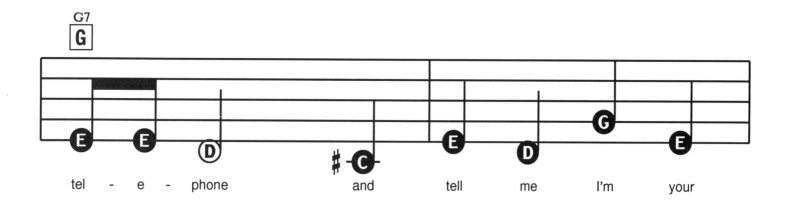

tel - e - phone and tell me I'm your

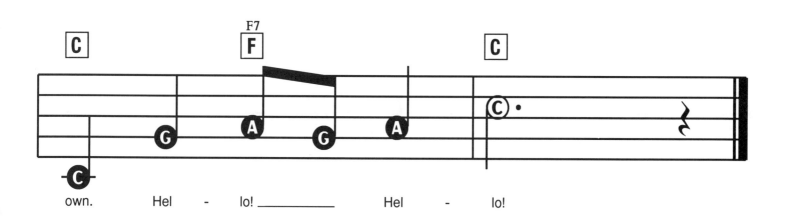

own. Hel - lo! _____ Hel - lo!

Ida, Sweet as Apple Cider

Words by Eddie Leonard
Music by Eddie Munson

Registration 3
Rhythm: Fox Trot or Swing

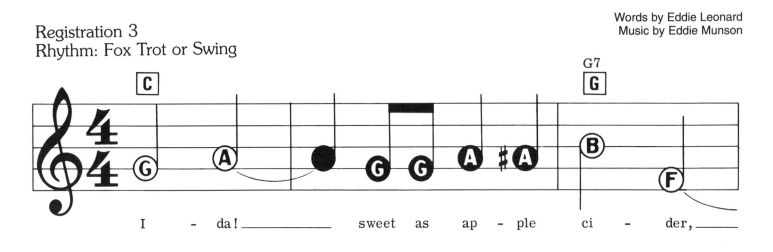

I - da! _____ sweet as ap - ple ci - der, _____

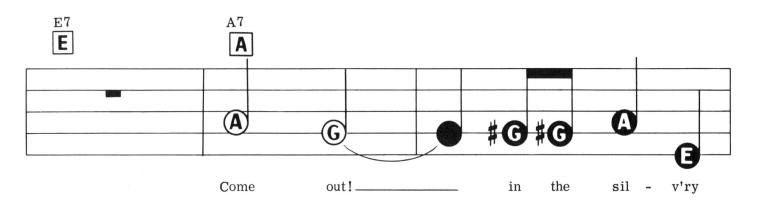

_____ Sweet - er _____ than all I know,

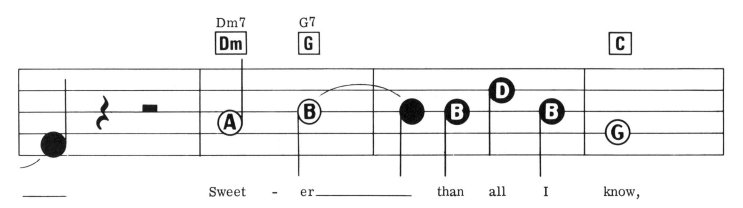

Come out! _____ in the sil - v'ry

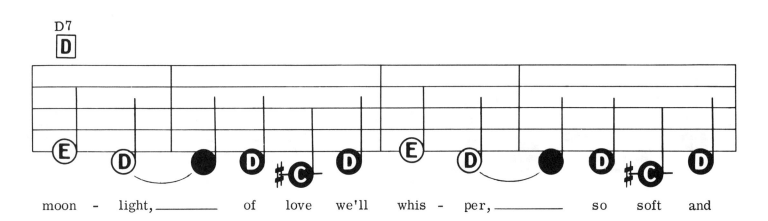

moon - light, _____ of love we'll whis - per, _____ so soft and

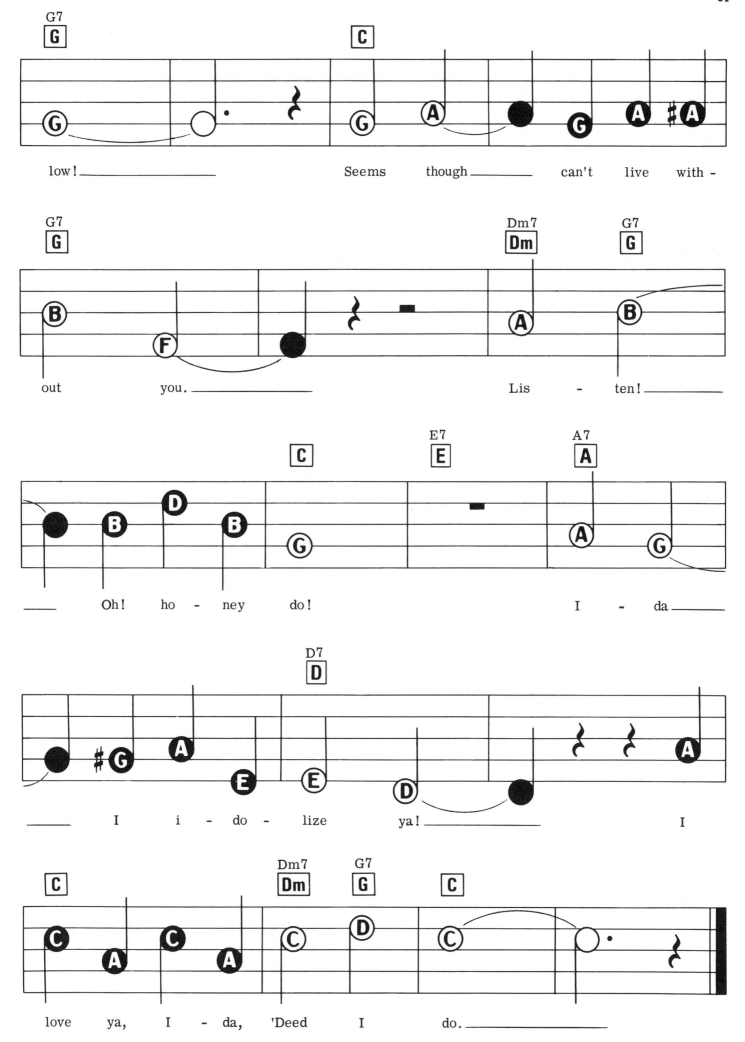

I Want a Girl
(Just Like the Girl That Married Dear Old Dad)

Registration 2
Rhythm: Swing or Jazz

Words by William Dillon
Music by Harry Von Tilzer

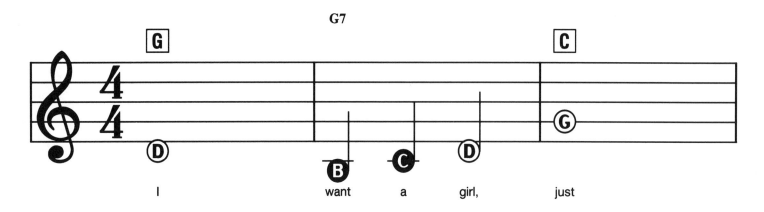

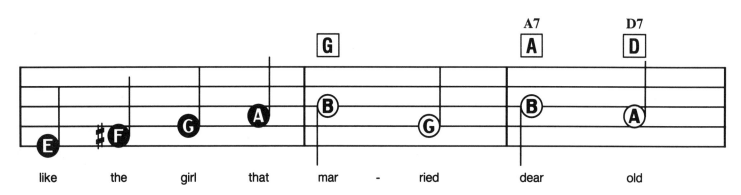

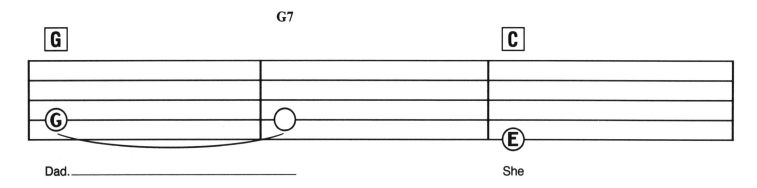

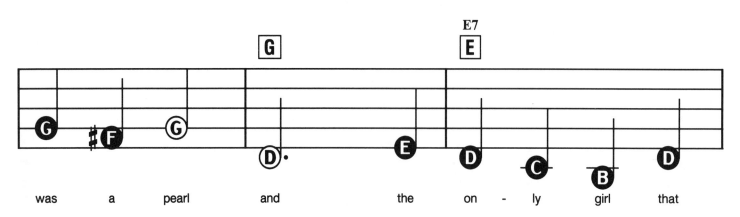

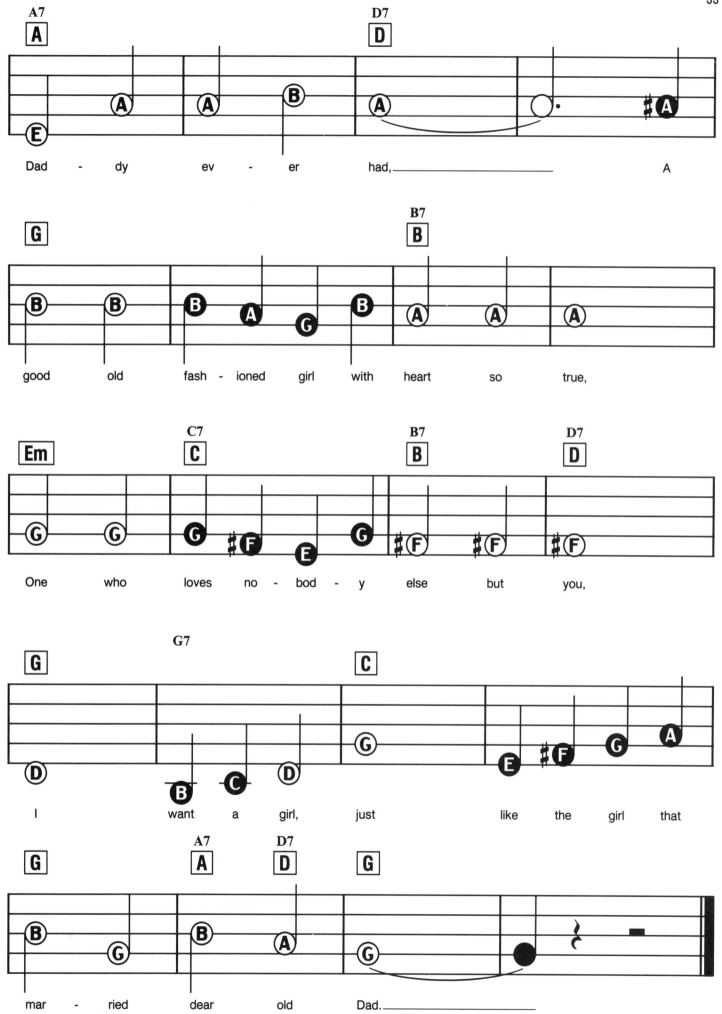

Pack Up Your Troubles in Your Old Kit Bag and Smile, Smile, Smile

Registration 4
Rhythm: March

Words by George Asaf
Music by Felix Powell

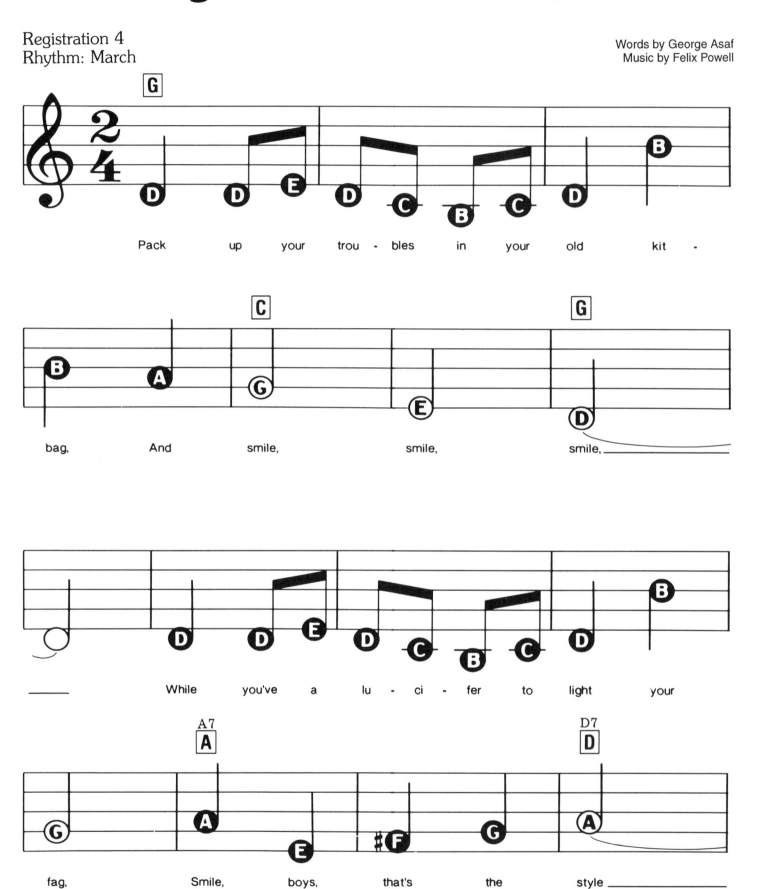

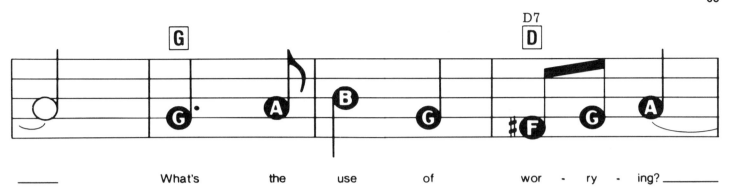

_____ What's the use of wor - ry - ing? _____

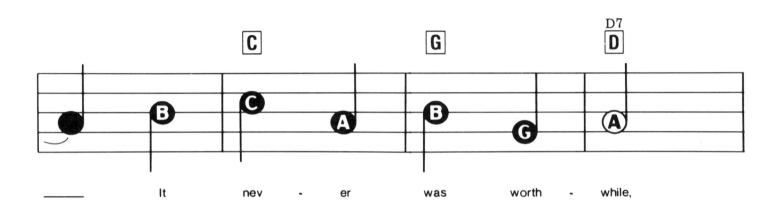

_____ It nev - er was worth - while,

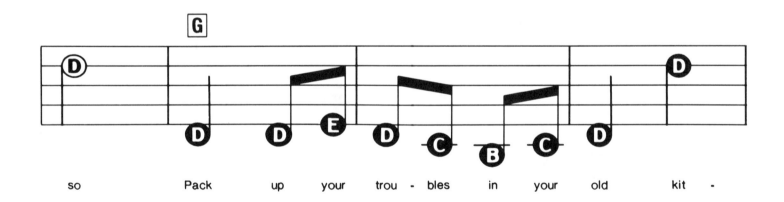

so Pack up your trou - bles in your old kit -

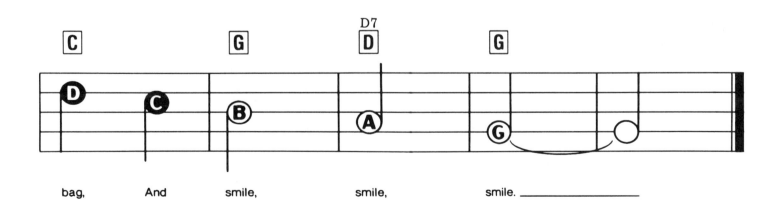

bag, And smile, smile, smile. _____

Poor Butterfly

Registration 1
Rhythm: Fox Trot or Swing

Words by John L. Golden
Music by Raymond Hubbell

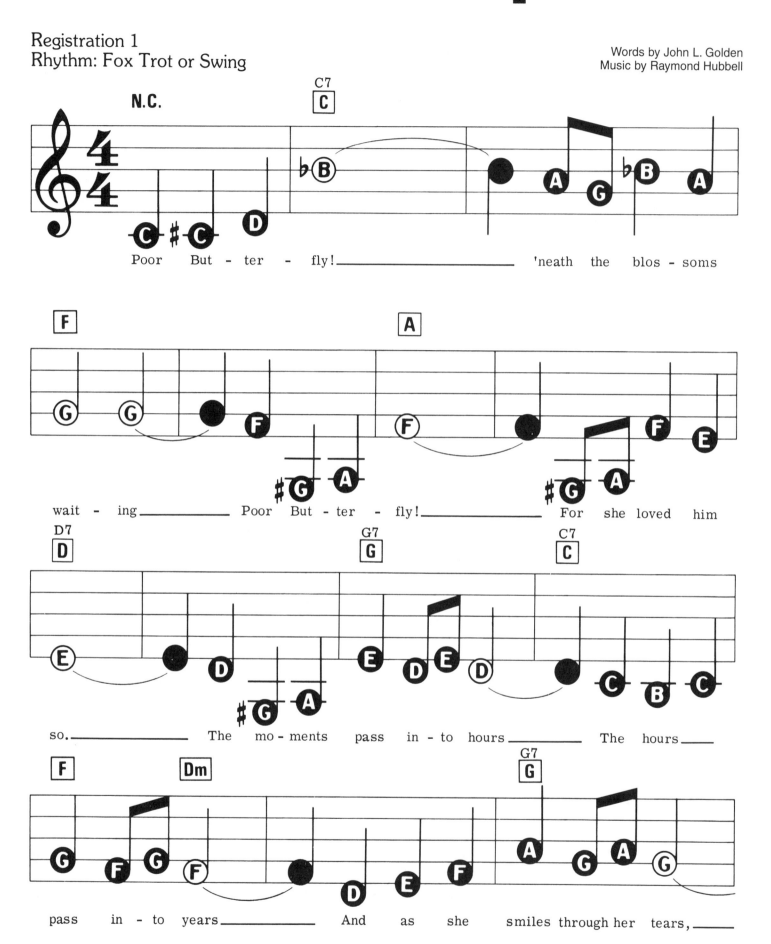

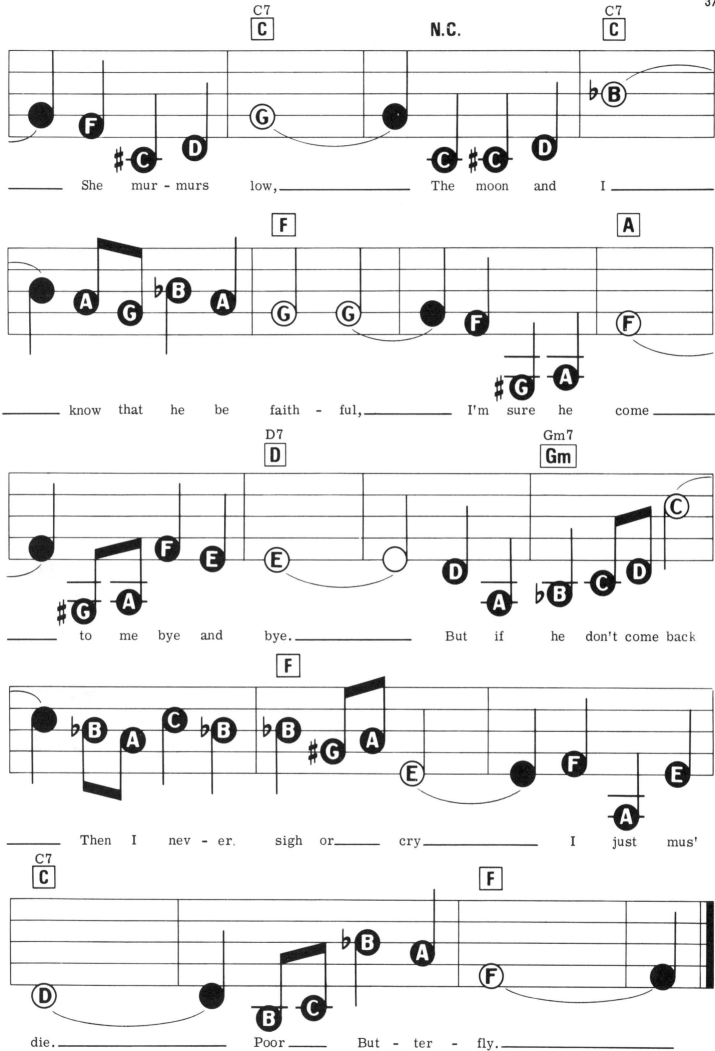

Pretty Baby

Registration 2
Rhythm: Swing

Words by Gus Kahn
Music by Egbert Van Alstyne and Tony Jackson

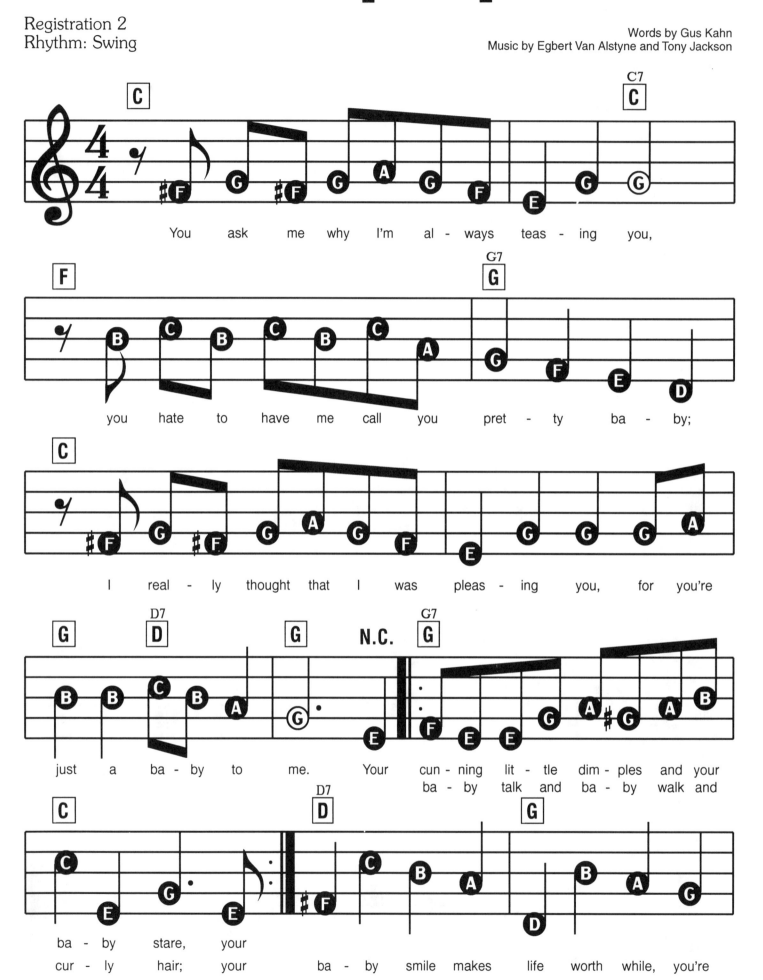

A Pretty Girl Is Like a Melody

Registration 8
Rhythm: Fox Trot or Ballad

Words and Music by
Irving Berlin

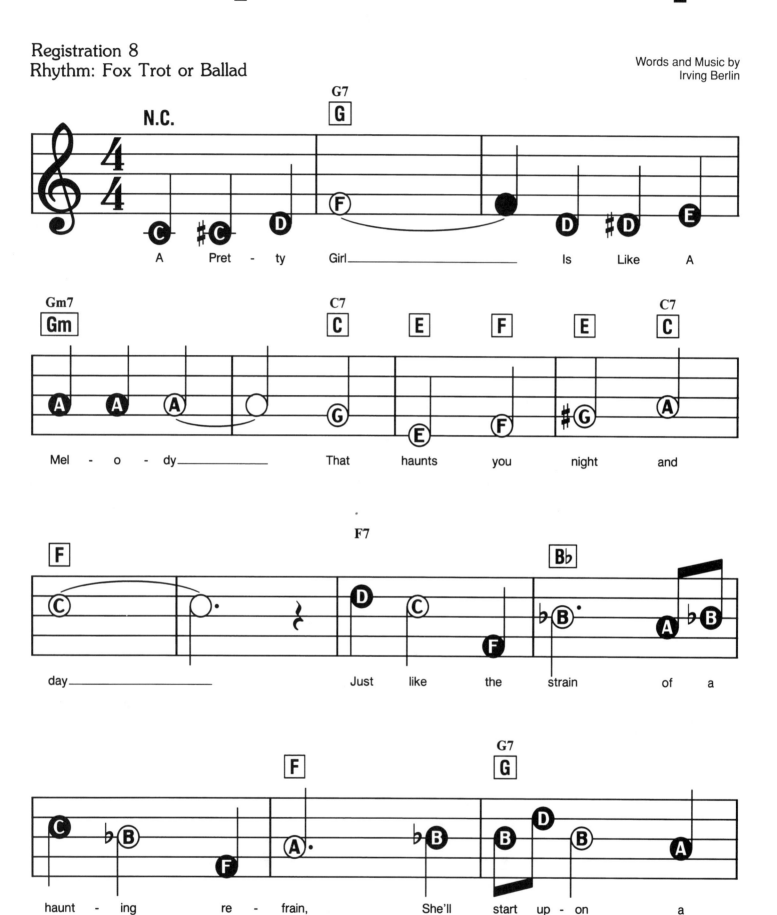

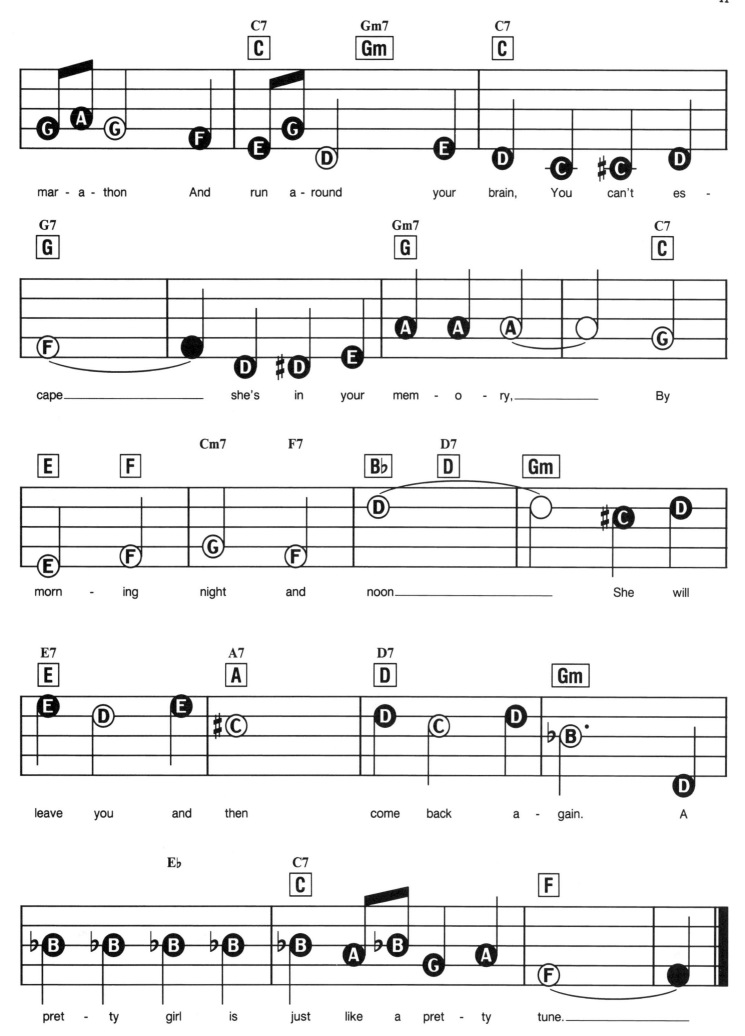

Put Your Arms Around Me, Honey

Registration 9
Rhythm: Fox Trot

Words by Junie McCree
Music by Albert Von Tilzer

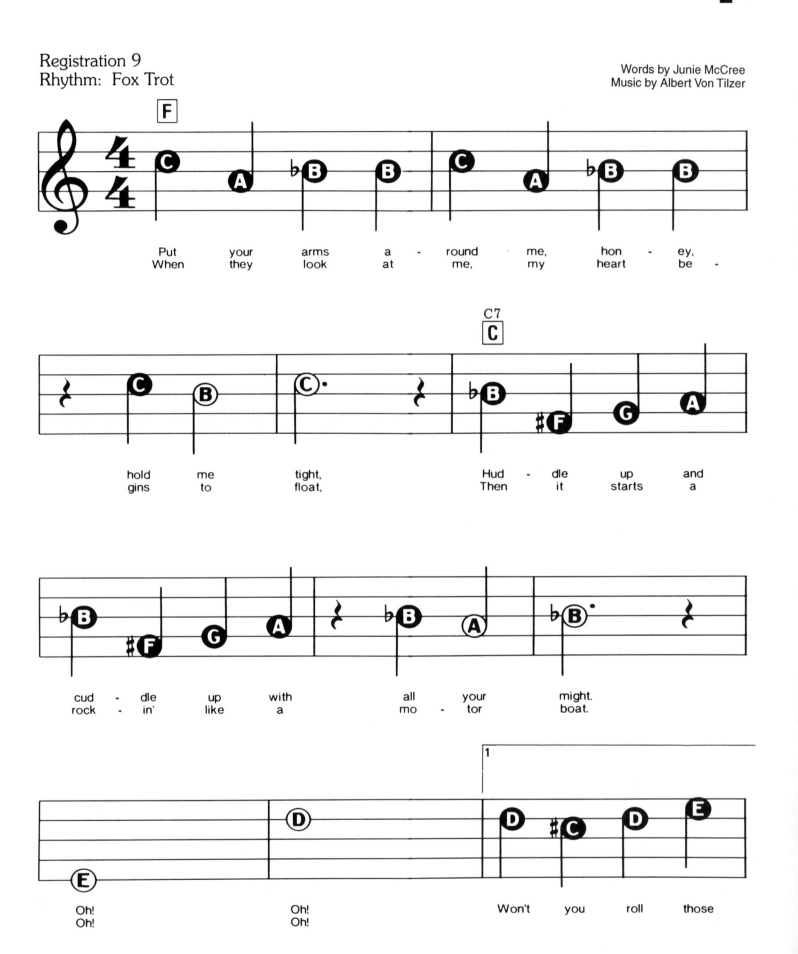

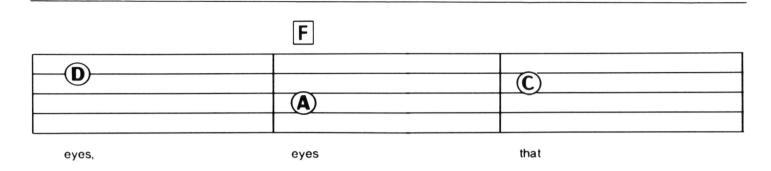

eyes,   eyes   that

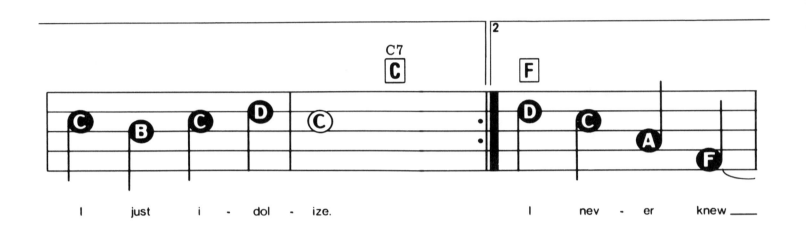

I just i - dol - ize.   I nev - er knew ____

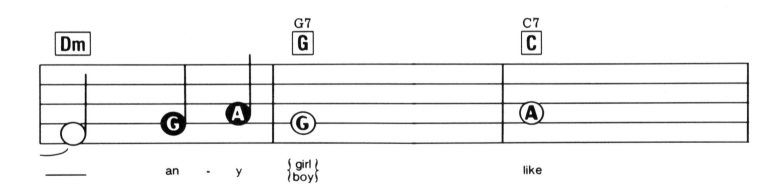

____ an - y {girl}{boy}   like

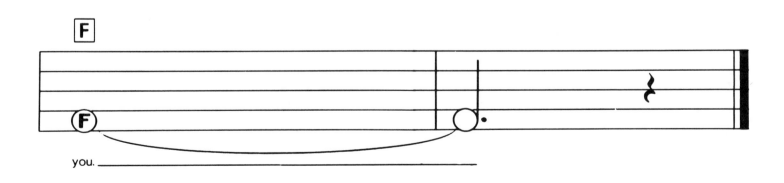

you. ____

Rock-A-Bye Your Baby
with a Dixie Melody

Registration 9
Rhythm: Fox Trot or Swing

Words by Sam M. Lewis and Joe Young
Music by Jean Schwartz

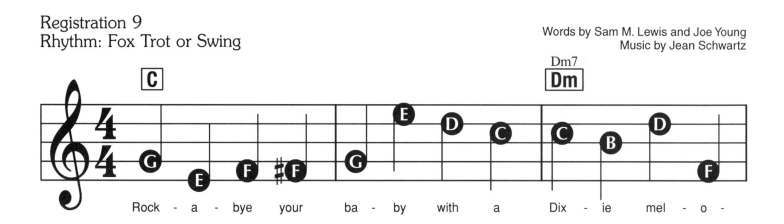

Rock - a - bye your ba - by with a Dix - ie mel - o -

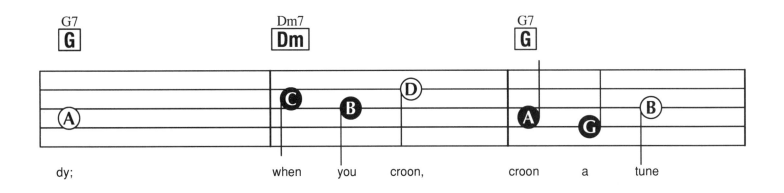

dy; when you croon, croon a tune

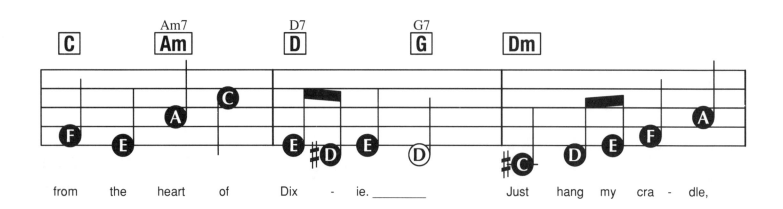

from the heart of Dix - ie. _____ Just hang my cra - dle,

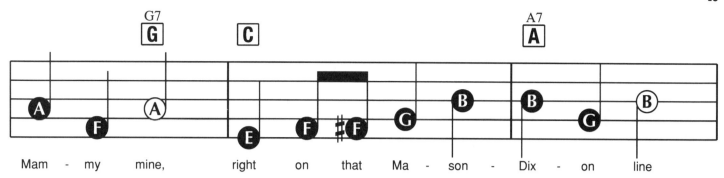

Mam - my mine, right on that Ma - son - Dix - on line

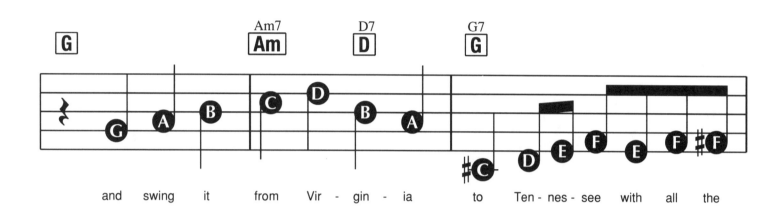

and swing it from Vir - gin - ia to Ten - nes - see with all the

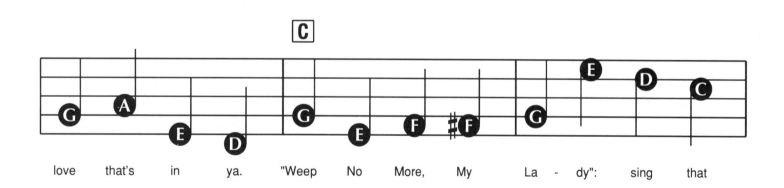

love that's in ya. "Weep No More, My La - dy": sing that

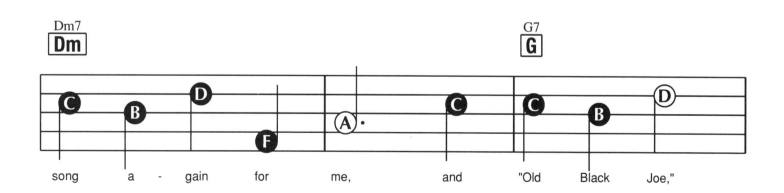

song a - gain for me, and "Old Black Joe,"

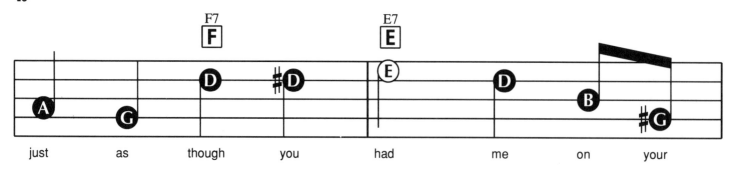

just   as   though   you   had   me   on   your

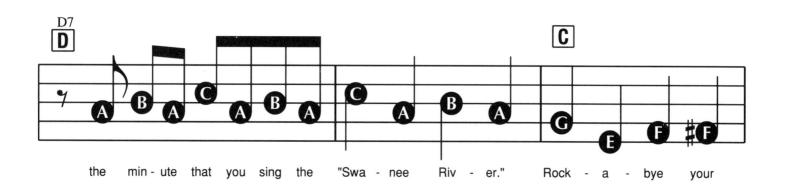

knee.   A   mil - lion   ba - by   kiss - es   I'll   de - liv - er

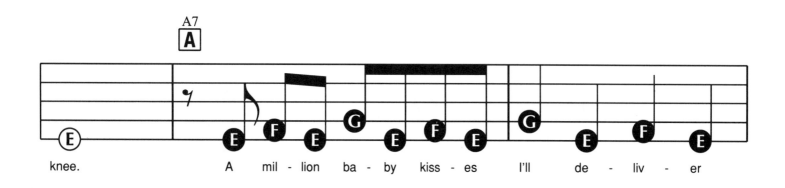

the   min - ute   that   you   sing   the   "Swa - nee   Riv - er."   Rock - a - bye   your

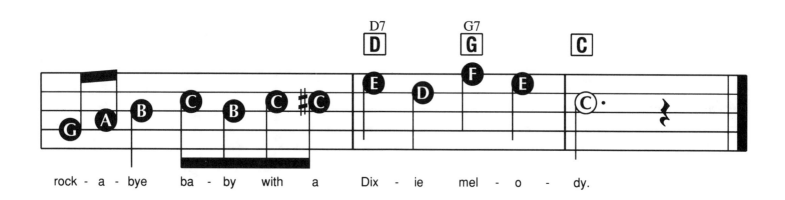

rock - a - bye   ba - by   with   a   Dix - ie   mel - o - dy.

Second Hand Rose

Registration 8
Rhythm: Fox Trot or Swing

Words by Grant Clarke
Music by James F. Hanley

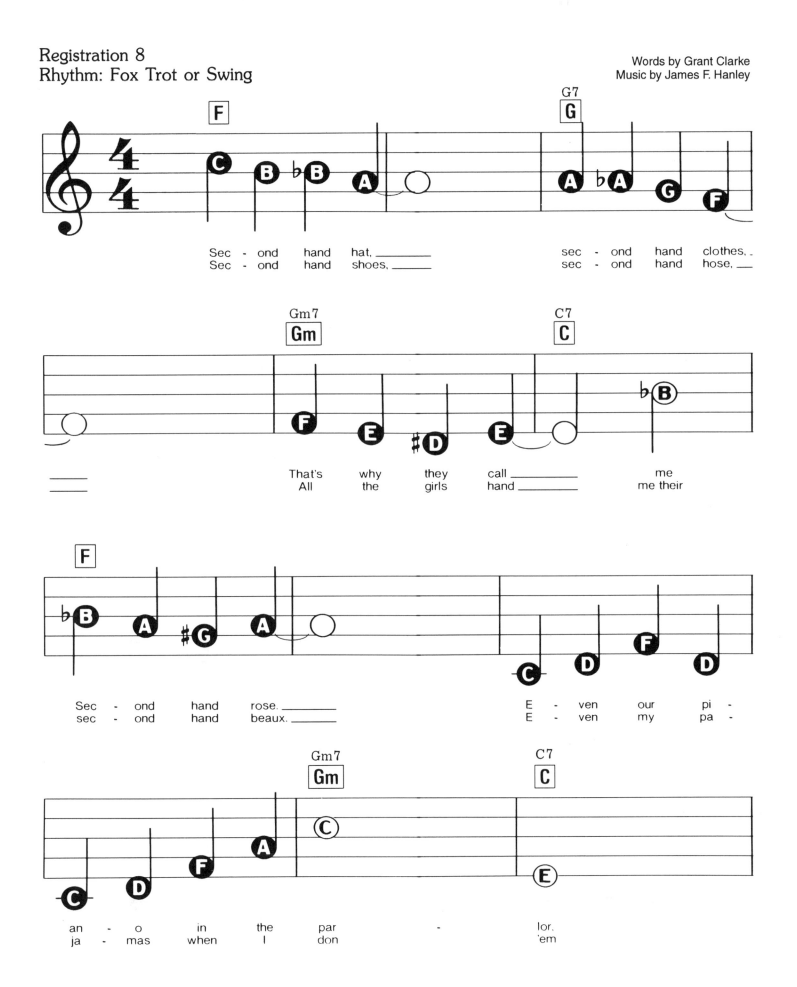

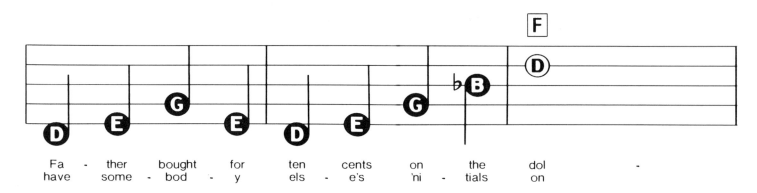

Fa - ther bought for ten cents on the dol - lar.
have some - bod - y els - e's 'ni - tials on 'em.

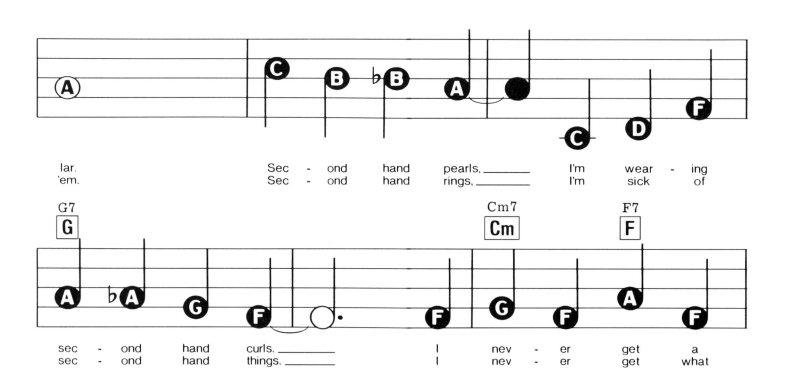

Sec - ond hand pearls, _____ I'm wear - ing
Sec - ond hand rings, _____ I'm sick of

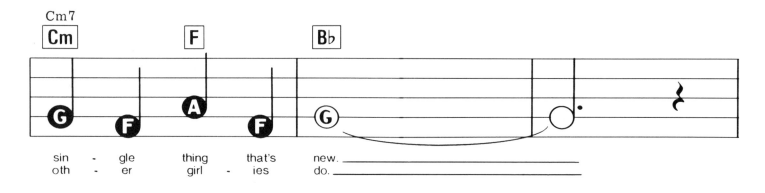

sec - ond hand curls. _____ I nev - er get a
sec - ond hand things. _____ I nev - er get what

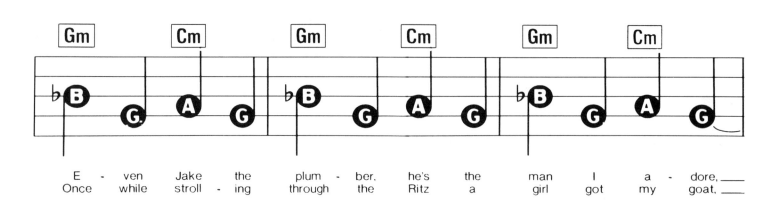

sin - gle thing that's new. _____
oth - er girl - ies do. _____

E - ven Jake the plum - ber, he's the man I a - dore, ____
Once while stroll - ing through the Ritz a girl got my goat, ____

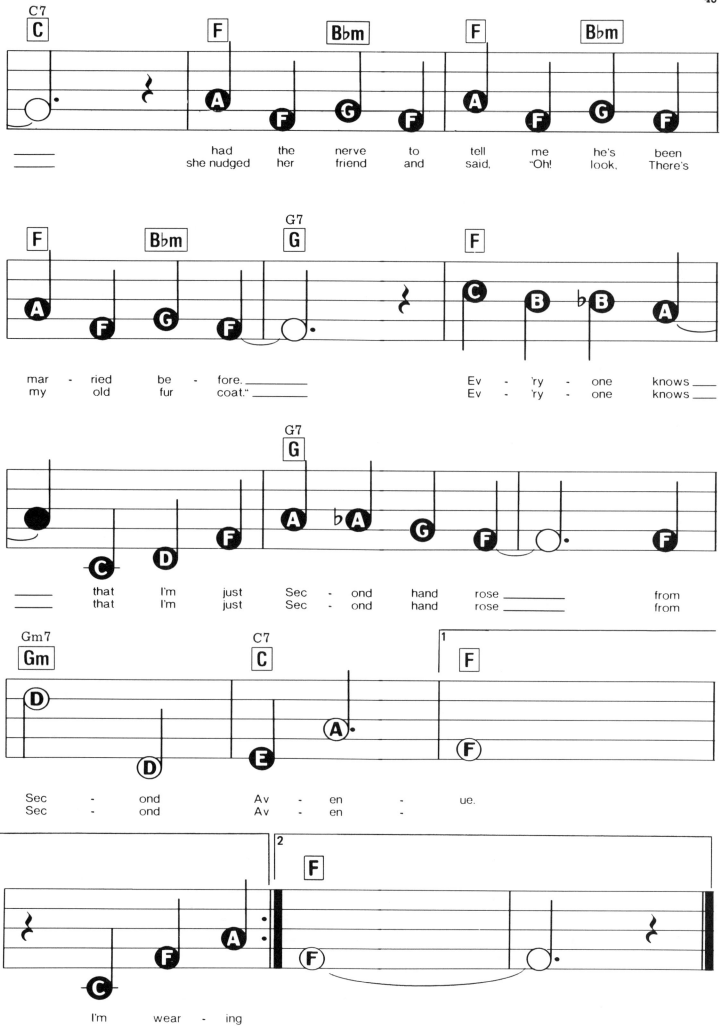

Some of These Days

Registration 1
Rhythm: Swing or Shuffle

Words and Music by
Shelton Brooks

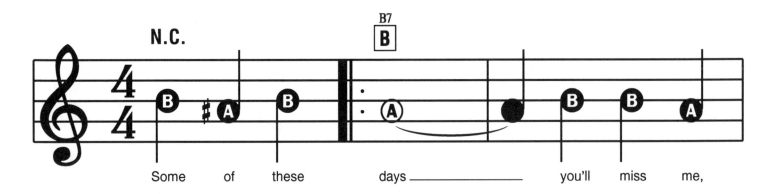

Some of these days _____ you'll miss me,

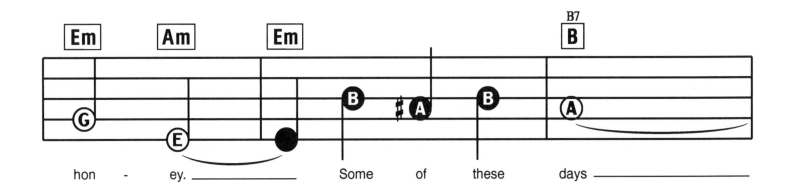

hon - ey. _____ Some of these days _____

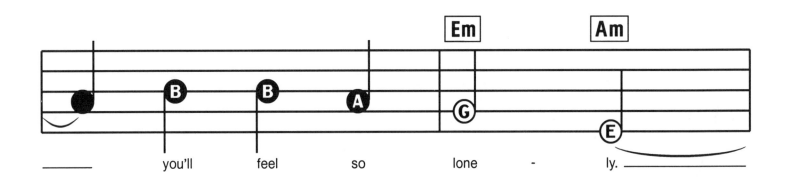

_____ you'll feel so lone - ly. _____

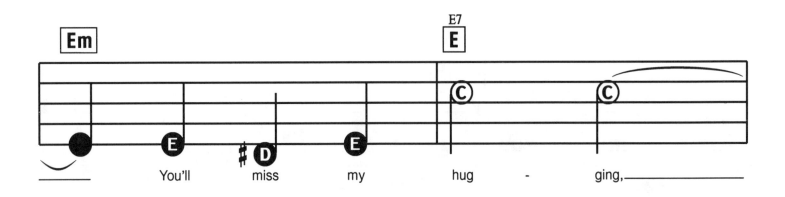

_____ You'll miss my hug - ging, _____

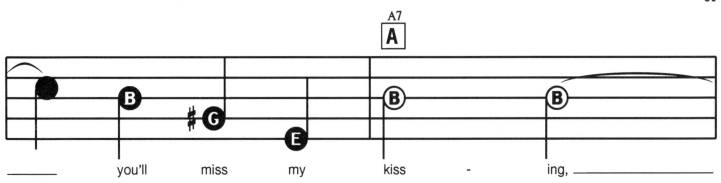

you'll   miss   my   kiss   -   ing, _____

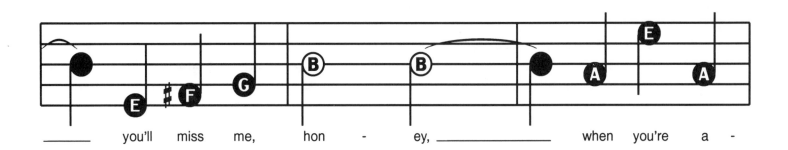

_____   you'll   miss   me,   hon   -   ey, _____   when   you're   a   -

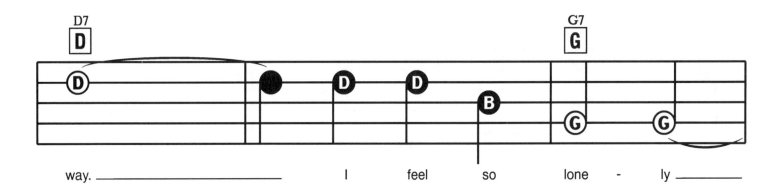

way. _____   I   feel   so   lone   -   ly _____

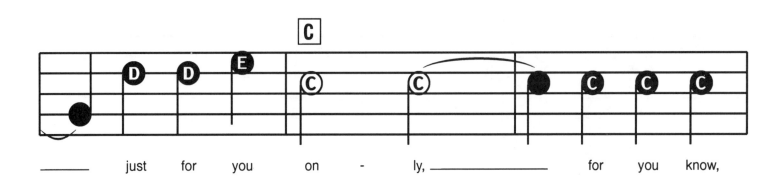

_____   just   for   you   on   -   ly, _____   for   you   know,

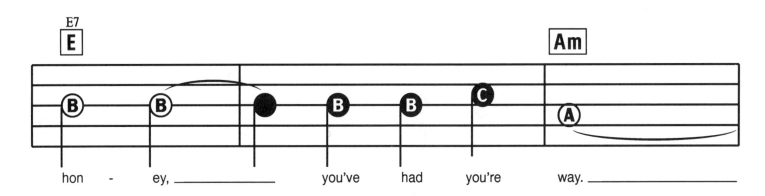

hon   -   ey, _____   you've   had   you're   way. _____

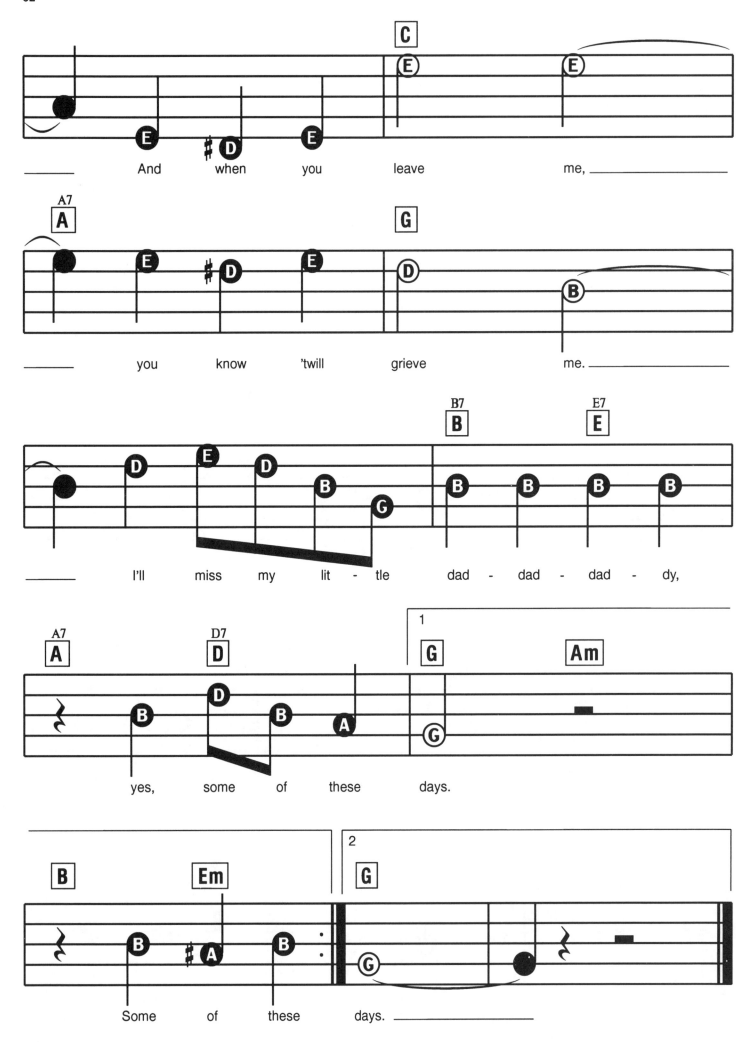

Under the Bamboo Tree

Registration 10
Rhythm: Fox Trot

Words and Music by Robert Cole
and J. Rosamond Johnson

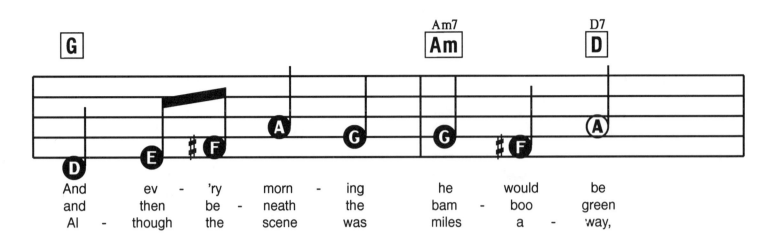

And ev - 'ry morn - ing he would be
and then be - neath the bam - boo green
Al - though the scene was miles a - way,

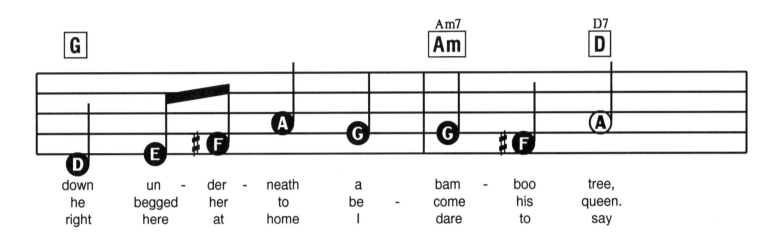

down un - der - neath a bam - boo tree,
he begged her to be - come his queen.
right here at home I dare to say

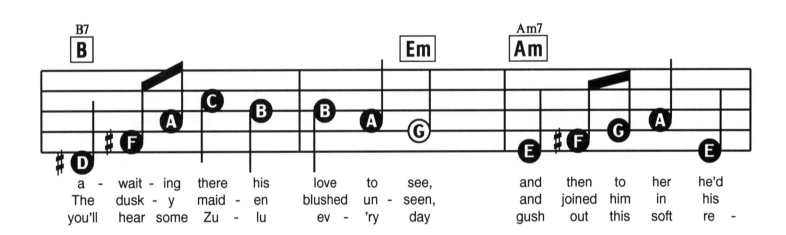

a - wait - ing there his love to see,
The dusk - y maid - en blushed un - seen,
you'll hear some Zu - lu ev - 'ry day

and then to her he'd
and joined him in his
gush out this soft re -

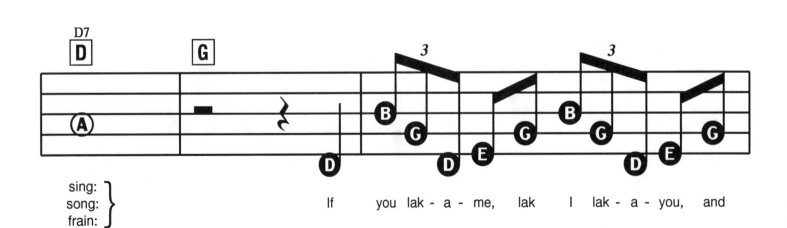

sing:
song: }
frain:

If you lak - a - me, lak I lak - a - you, and

55

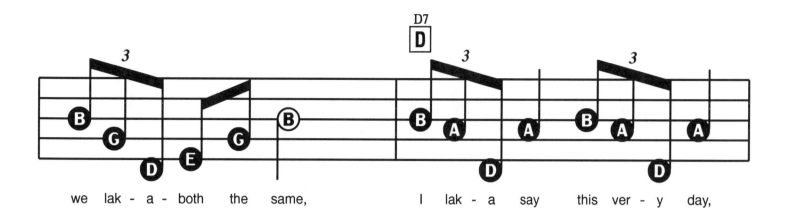

we lak - a - both the same, I lak - a say this ver - y day,

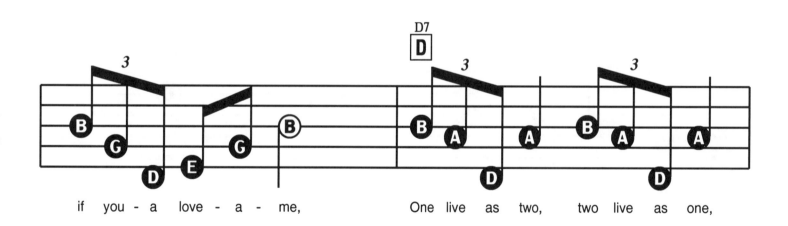

I lak - a change your name. _____ 'Cause I love - a - you and love - a - you true, and

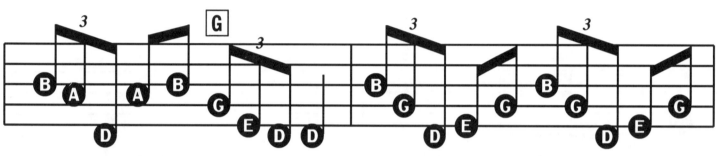

if you - a love - a - me, One live as two, two live as one,

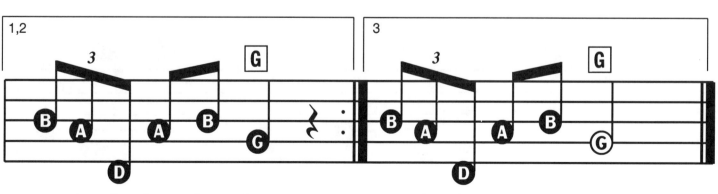

un - der the bam - boo tree.   un - der the bam - boo tree.

Swanee

Registration 9
Rhythm: Fox Trot or Swing

Words by Irving Caesar
Music by George Gershwin

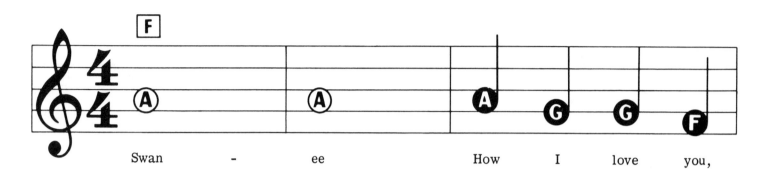

Swan - ee   How   I   love   you,

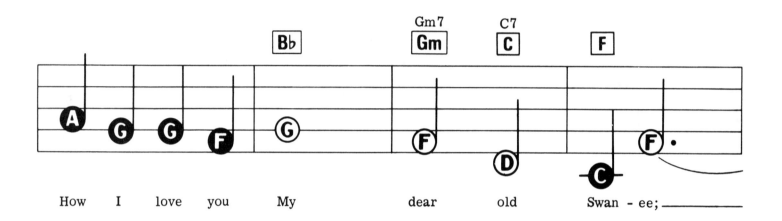

How   I   love   you   My   dear   old   Swan - ee; _____

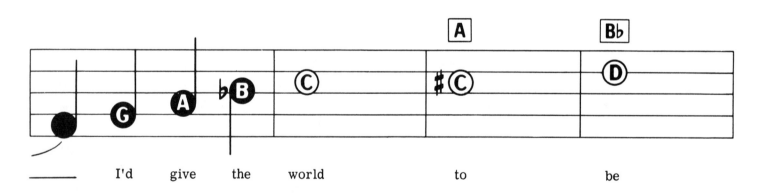

_____   I'd   give   the   world   to   be

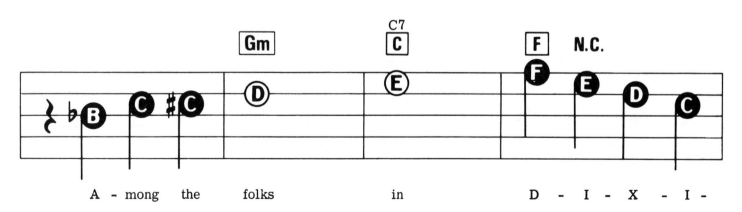

A - mong   the   folks   in   D - I - X - I -

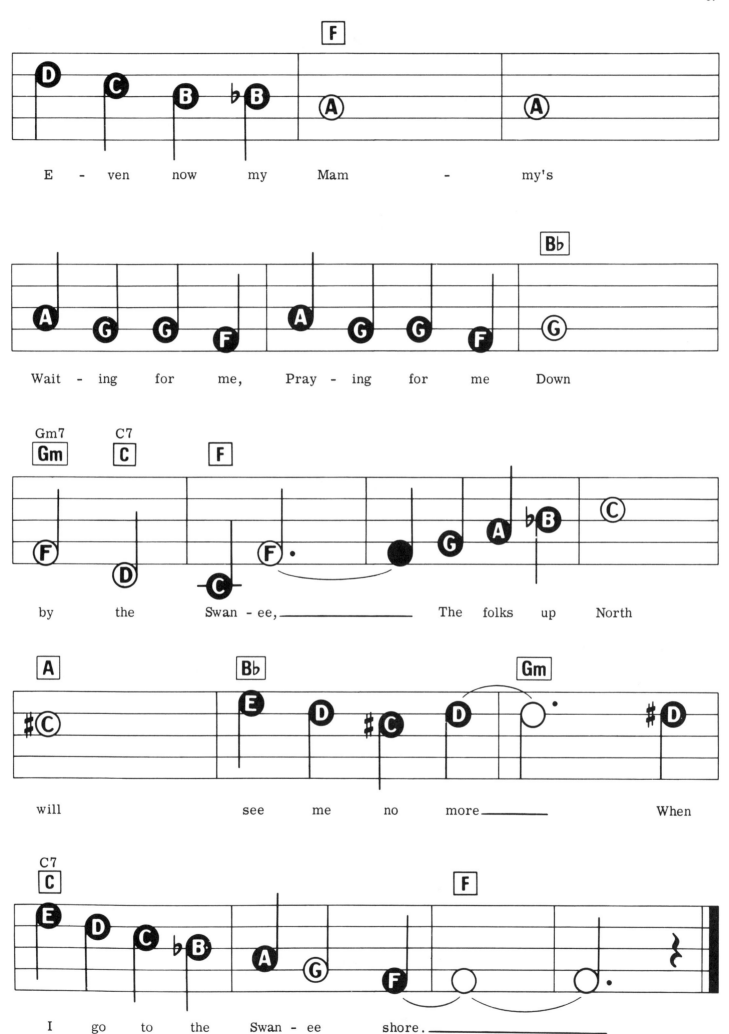

'Way Down Yonder in New Orleans

Registration 7
Rhythm: Swing

Words and Music by Henry Creamer and
J. Turner Layton

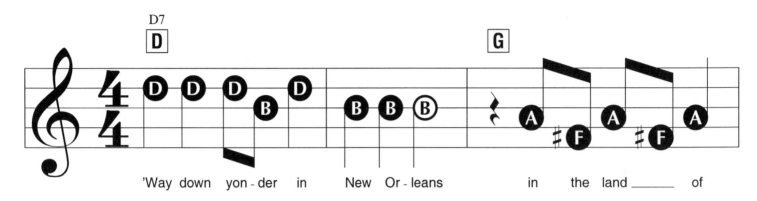

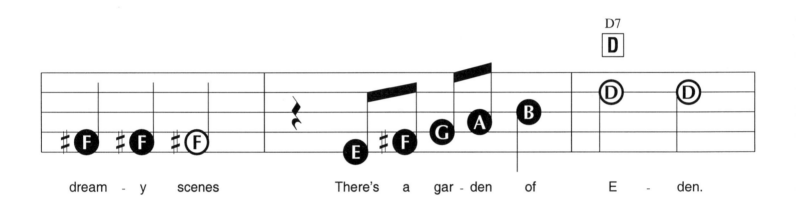

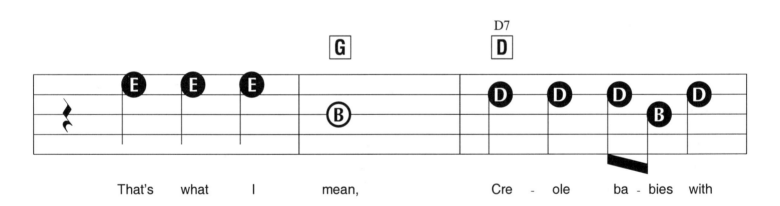

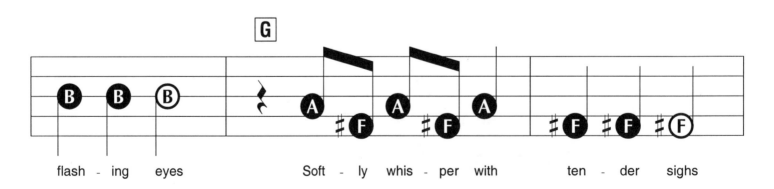

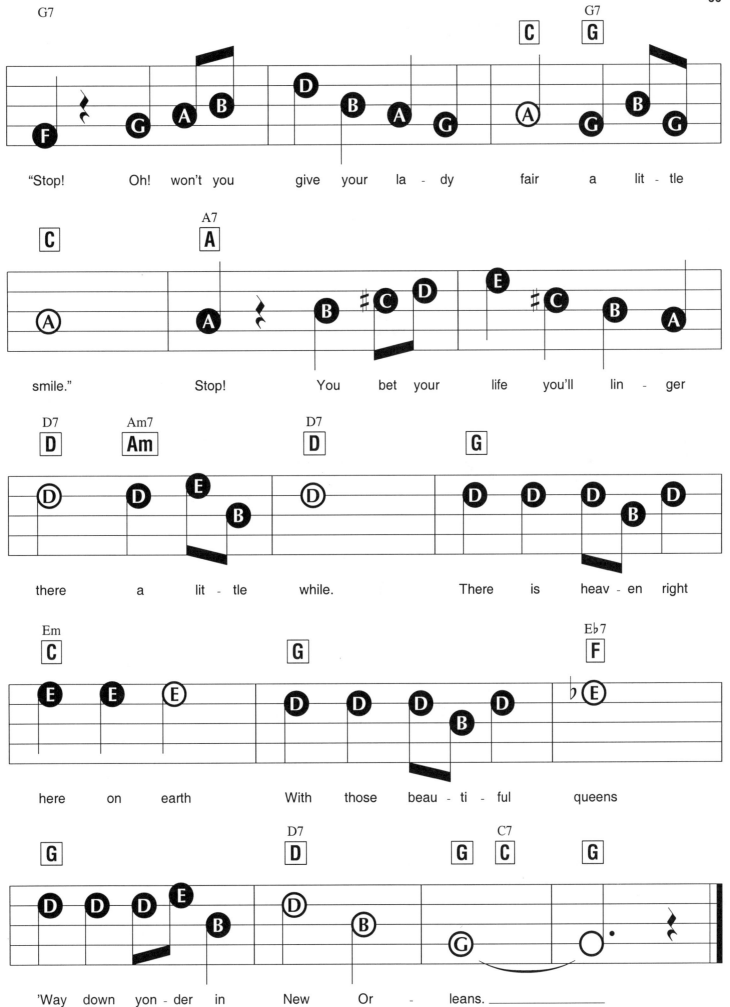

When My Baby Smiles at Me

Registration 1
Rhythm: Fox Trot or Swing

Words and Music by Harry Von Tilzer, Andrew B. Sterling,
Bill Munro and Ted Lewis

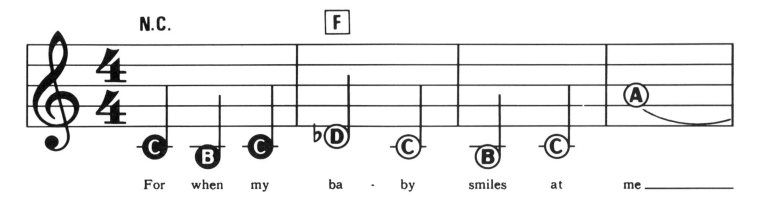

For when my ba - by smiles at me _____

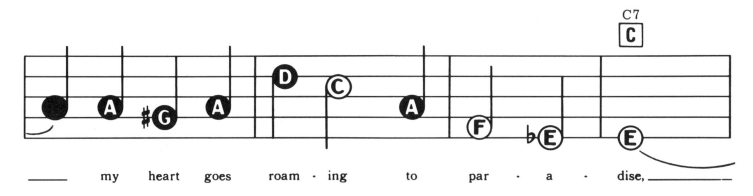

_____ my heart goes roam - ing to par - a - dise, _____

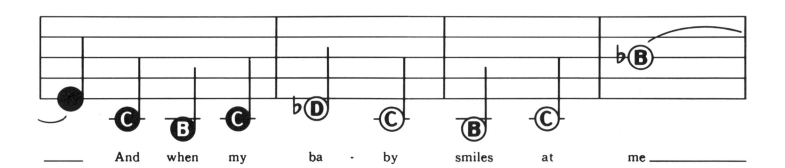

_____ And when my ba - by smiles at me _____

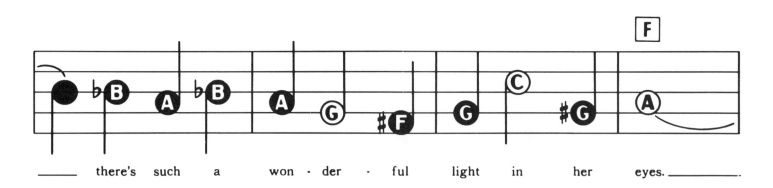

_____ there's such a won - der - ful light in her eyes. _____

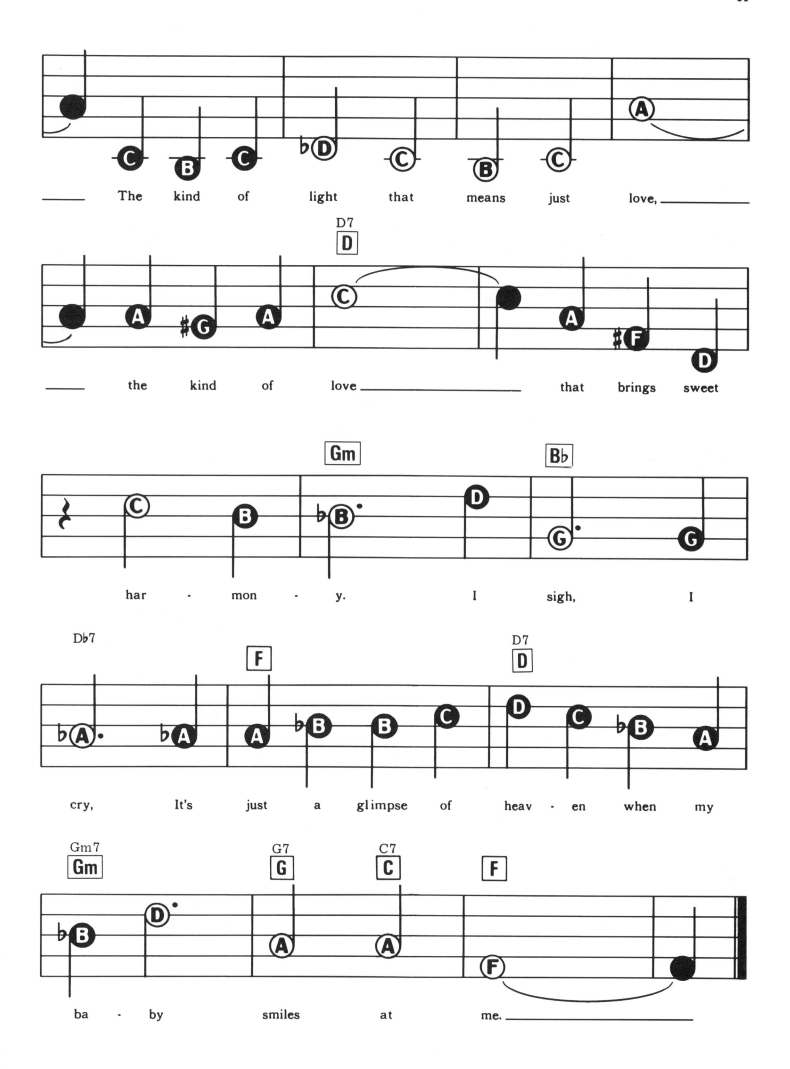

When You Wore a Tulip
(And I Wore a Big Red Rose)

Registration 9
Rhythm: Fox Trot or Pops

Words by Jack Mahoney
Music by Percy Wenrich

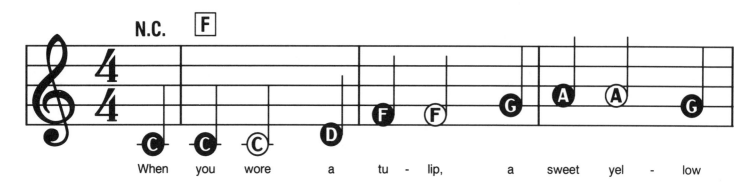

When you wore a tu - lip, a sweet yel - low

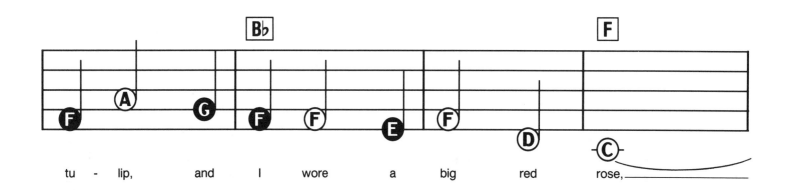

tu - lip, and I wore a big red rose,

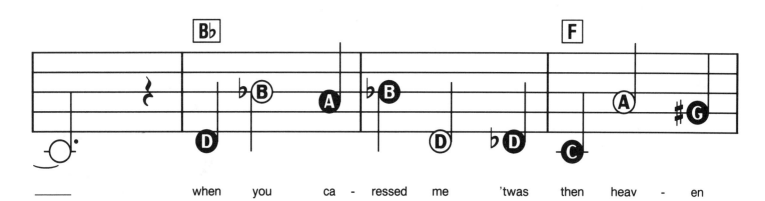

when you ca - ressed me 'twas then heav - en

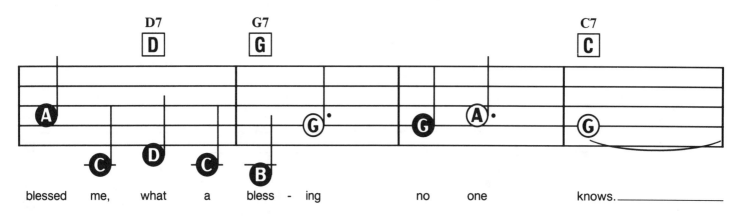

blessed me, what a bless - ing no one knows.

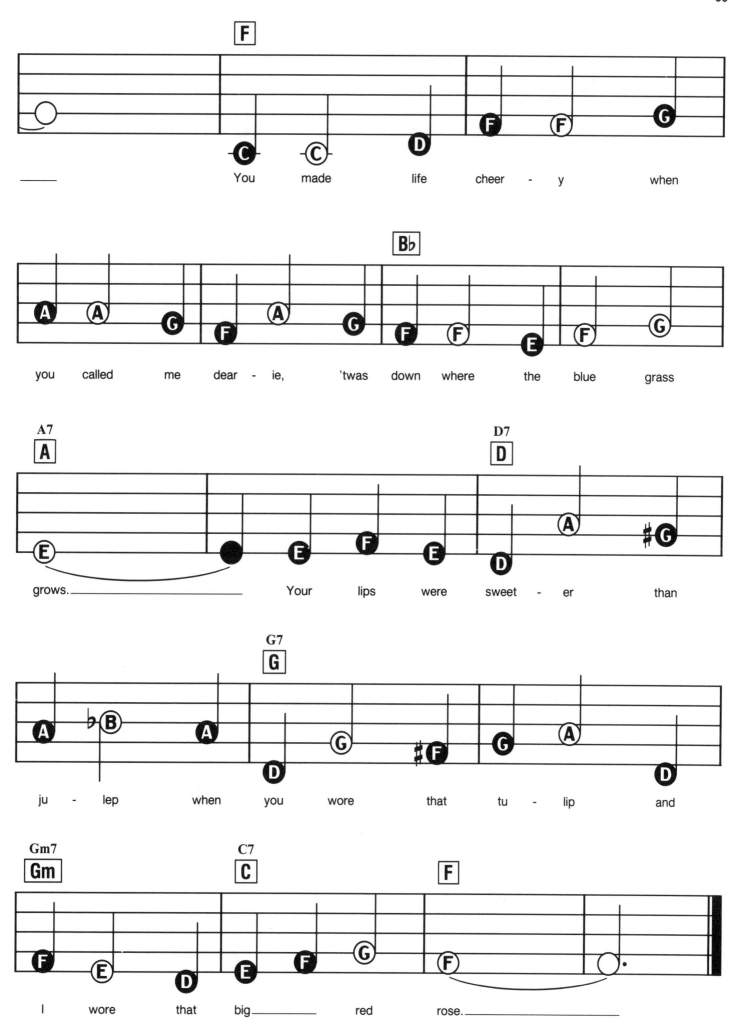

Registration Guide

- Match the Registration number on the song to the corresponding numbered category below. Select and activate an instrumental sound available on your instrument.

- Choose an automatic rhythm appropriate to the mood and style of the song. (Consult your Owner's Guide for proper operation of automatic rhythm features.)

- Adjust the tempo and volume controls to comfortable settings.

Registration

1	Flute, Pan Flute, Jazz Flute
2	Clarinet, Organ
3	Violin, Strings
4	Brass, Trumpet
5	Synth Ensemble, Accordion, Brass
6	Pipe Organ, Harpsichord
7	Jazz Organ, Vibraphone, Vibes, Electric Piano, Jazz Guitar
8	Piano, Electric Piano
9	Trumpet, Trombone, Clarinet, Saxophone, Oboe
10	Violin, Cello, Strings